G000049021

"Time is something which prevents everything from happening at once."

Bruce Lee

Anthology

Films and Fighting

**A collection of writings and illustrations,
from the pages of K.O.A. magazine,
with additional material
by Paul Crompton,
former editor.**

Paul H. Crompton Ltd.

First published 1999

(C) Copyright Paul Crompton &
Paul H. Crompton Ltd. 1998

All rights reserved.
No part of this book may be
reproduced in any way whatsoever
without written permission of the
copyright holders.

ISBN 1 874250 90 1

Acknowledgements...

The following companies originally contributed the information and photographs to the issues of "Karate & Oriental Arts" magazine from which the contents of this anthology are mainly taken.

Cathay Films, Dennis Davidson Associates Ltd., EMI Films, Enterprise Pictures, Golden Harvest, Rank Film Distributors, 20th Century Fox, Hong Kong Urban Council, Warner Brothers.

The editor would also like to thank the following people for their contributions, direct or indirect to keeping K.O.A. magazine on its feet for twenty-two years and providing information. If I have left anyone out, my apologies.

Jon Alexander
John Anderson
Steve Arneil
Alick Au
Richard Batchelor
Nino Bernardo
Pauline Bindra
Bob Breen
John Brooke
Steve Cattle
Ji Jian Chang
Joseph Cheng
William Cheung
Mantak Chia
M.J. Clapton
Rolf Clausnitzer
Danny Connor
John Darwen
James DeMile
Sean Dervan
'Ticky' Donovan
Brian Dossett
Alan Ellerton
Paul Elston
Keinosuke Enoeda
Michael Finn
Ronald Forrester
Bruce Frantzis
Derek Frearson
Austin Goh
Jay Gluck
Beth Grossman
Charles Hanson
Larry Hartsell

Norma Harvey
Hans Hesselmann
Tom Hibbert
Nobuko Hirose
B.S. Huan
Dan Inosanto
Don Jacobs
Lajos Jakab
Wally Jay
Derek Jones
Victor Kan
Hirokasu Kanazawa
Keith Kernspecht
Hrut Keshishian
Gunji Koizumi
Samuel Kwok
Simon Lau
Rene Latosa
Keith Lebihan
Ah Loi Lee
Mark Lemon
James Lew
Peder Lund
Charles Mack
Ian MacLaren
Cass Magda
Roland Maroteaux
David Mitchell
Roger Moore
Tom Morris
Bill Newman
Terry O'Neill
Len Palmer
Henri Plee

Thierry Plee
G.F. Scott
Walter Seaton
James Self
David Shaw
Jeffrey Somers
James Shortt
Masafumi Shiomitsu
John Smith
Tom Smithson
Bob Stannells
Andrew Stoker
Tatsuo Suzuki
Chris Thompson
J.S. Thompson
Leung Ting
Frances Toner
Ho Bun Un
Dominique Valera
Bob Wall
Donn Warrener
Gunther Weil
Paul Whitrod
Bryn Williams
Jim Wilson
Colin Whitaker
Curtis Wong
Greco Wong
Jan Wright
Ken Wright
Jwing-Ming Yang
Theresa Yang
Rebac Zoran

For help with this volume I particularly thank
Larry Hartsell
Cass Magda
Bob Breen
Rex Features
Steve Taplin
Rene Latosa
Bill Newman
Chris Sutton
Jan Wright
James DeMile
Curtis Wong
Brian Klingborg
Carlton International Media Ltd.

From the Editor,...

It is over thirty-two years since the first martial arts magazine to be published in England made its appearance. It was called "Karate & Oriental Arts", and I was the editor. In due course the title was abbreviated to K.O.A. It ran for about twenty-two years, and then I closed it down. Running a magazine is tough work and I had had enough.

Over the years people have phoned me or written, asking if K.O.A. could be revived. No . Instead, I decided to produce a book based on articles which appeared in the publication, devoted to the man whose influence has by far been the greatest in promoting and maintaining the general public's interest in martial arts. That man was, and we can in effect say still is, Bruce Lee.

This compromise with readers, of a Bruce Lee Anthology, will I hope prove to be a trip down memory lane for all the middle-aged K.O.A. readers and provide an insight for younger readers into some of the influences which shaped the present martial arts scene.

Lee's truly meteoric impact on martial arts since the 1970's can indeed be compared with such a planetary event. Up to that time, public awareness of the arts was growing, slowly, at a relatively pedestrian pace. Bruce Lee brought himself and Kung fu, aided by David Carradine's television series, right into people's living rooms. Overnight, Karate clubs, devoted to the Japanese art, suddenly acquired Kung fu status and eager students crammed into training halls like the proverbial sardines. Fortunes were made by some enterprising figures in the martial arts world, not to mention in the fields of film and television; Lee had handed them a blank cheque.

In the area of martial arts training and theory, Bruce Lee also produced a paradox. On the one hand he maintained that the "classical mess", by which he meant old, traditional training methods which he saw as out-dated, were a drag on a person's martial arts development. Be spontaneous, was his suggestion. On the other hand, how can one be spontaneous without previous training? How can you play spontaneous jazz if you have not learned how to play in the first place? It was something of a puzzle for students to figure out.

Lee's own avowed chief influence was Wing Chun Kung fu. Without it, would he have been able to develop his own Jeet Kune Do, which in itself is something of a "tradition", among some teachers, twenty-five years after his untimely death? It makes you think.

This anthology has developed. First it was simply an idea, of sharing K.O.A.'s publications with former and new readers. As I slowly put the contents together it took me down memory lane too. I recalled with some humour the article we printed about the con man in Germany who ripped off martial arts students in Europe anxious to learn about Bruce Lee's methods . When I originally wrote the article, I could not help referring to the Taoist sayings attributed to Lao-tze as they fitted the context perfectly. Though the con itself was absolutely nothing to laugh about, the apposite sayings could not be seen as anything but humorous. There was the Chinese sage, applying his wisdom to a modern day situation, thousands of years later.

For me the Bruce Lee films have not worn well. All these years later, it is something of a mystery to me why such films were so intoxicating to the fans. One sees now that they could have been so much better and one reflects that the star's talents were in a way wasted in them. Intellectually it is clear why the things that happened did happen but it is nevertheless regrettable. Though born in San Francisco, Bruce Lee was really a native of Hong Kong, but it is a pity that he did not grow up on the West Coast, harbouring the same ambitions, and meeting much better film makers in his youth. As it is, we owe his stardom in part to men who were making films on a shoe-string to please a cinematically uncritical audience.

Some of Lee's pupils such as Dan Inosanto and some of their pupils I remembered meeting from time to time during the boom days. They were always courteous and helpful, amazingly laid back considering the pressure they were under. It was only when I met Curtis Wong and James Lew in London and then later in Los Angeles that I began to feel at ease with this West Coast phenomenon.

I also remembered Mark Lemon, an Englishman who seemed to know more about the Bruce Lee scene than anyone else I have ever met; more than Bruce Lee and Dan Inosanto put together. Then there were the luckless journalists, searching for information to write about Bruce Lee, not knowing whether a nunchaku was for eating rice or waving. I remembered the dozens of fans, dying to look like Bruce Lee, think like Bruce Lee, learn what Bruce Lee learned.

I hope that readers can get enjoyment, above all, from this publication, rather than just knowledge or material for more controversy. This I say not from any disrespect towards the subjects, but because it was a very long time ago.

Contents

INTRODUCTION

My own life, along with the lives of hundreds of thousands of other people, has been influenced very much by the martial arts. In fact, since the end of the second world war in 1945, one could say that the growth and spread of the martial arts has been a miniature replica of some of the changes in society as a whole.

These changes include the breaking down of geographical and cultural boundaries, the massive expansions in media communication, and in recent years the explosion of the inter-net. In addition, we have witnessed a breakdown in individ-ual discipline, in personal relationships and a desire for, amounting to an assumed right to, instant gratification. It is as though the possibility of communication at the touch of a but-ton were a signal that everything should be available at the touch of a wish button.

In the martial arts, we have moved from a situation in which to obtain a black belt or first dan in judo or karate for instance required years of hard training and a tough exam, to a position in which a black belt could virtually be bought. This is not uni-versally true of course, but at one time it would have been unthinkable. This is a facet of the instant gratification image.

In a similar vein, the availability of videos showing how a martial art is done by an expert has led to a mushrooming of young "talents" whose experience with a teacher can be measured in hours rather than years, and to martial artists who can talk about, but who have little fundamental ground-ing in, the system they have chosen.

There is little point in belly-aching about this. As already said, it is a sign of the changed times, and is probably true about many other walks of life. There are few martial arts disciplines more vulnerable to this problem than Jeet Kune Do, (JKD), the name Bruce Lee chose for his own approach to fighting methods and philosophy. It centres around, in the public mind, the notion that if you let yourself be tied down to a traditional method of training, you will get stuck in routines which will limit your performance and development. This notion has been taken out of context by people who saw it as a quick way to claim expertise in a "style" produced by the most famous martial artist of the century. From the inability to face disciplined training, for whatever reason, such people have hit on the idea of posing as teachers of JKD with little or no basic training in any martial art at all.

Though still a young man when he died, Bruce Lee had spent thousands of hours training, studying, writing and re-writing his methods, as well as starring in films, starting a family and doing his best to keep things together. It was with such an arduous past behind him that the star produced his JKD basic ideas. He was not born with them in his hand. Compare his efforts with those of the microdots who believe they can emulate him simply by dragging a cloak over their heads called Jeet Kune Do. They should call their "system" the "I-am-too-lazy-to-go-through-the-discipline-style", and leave it at that.

I have written about my first hearing the name Bruce Lee a little later on. But in 1966 I started a magazine, with no publishing or financial training behind me, and refused to let it fail, even under the most difficult circumstances, such as when a printer let me down and I took the magazine, still in sheet form, and guillotined and bound it by hand at home in the living room, helped by my long-suffering wife.

The boom in those days, or rather the smouldering firework, was Karate. Hard to believe it now, but the word was almost unknown. Kung fu *was* unknown. I used to get into my old van, loaded up with magazines, and call at newsagents asking them to take K.O.A. on to their shelves for sale or return. This went on for some years. "Karate & Oriental Arts" (K.O.A.) grew in page size and page numbers. Wholesale newsagents began to accept it. It grew in size again. I would go to tournaments with my pencil and notebook in one hand and camera in the other to get material to publish. People sent in articles and photographs, we had a little advertising revenue, and in 1968 began to publish a few books. Then, Bruce Lee happened. Let me say it again, for the record. Bruce Lee happened. Just like that. Out of nowhere it seemed, and everything changed for me, and for hundreds and thousands of other people. Suddenly, K.O.A. was in demand. It did not matter what we published. Everyone wanted a magazine with martial arts in it. Our circulation shot up. We were not alone. Publishers crept out of the woodwork with an eye for a good thing when they saw it. Photographs of Bruce Lee were appearing time and again; not new ones, but the same ones, over and over. Fans bought anything with a photograph or sketch of Bruce in it. I was dumbfounded, almost. It was my first encounter with fan(atics) of any description.

At first the martial arts community too was shell-shocked, but they soon got over it and joined in the frenzy of packing students into their training halls. A few questionable characters occasionally turned up for training, I heard, anxious to learn ways of beating people into a pulp without too much effort.

A man was murdered in what the press called a Karate Killing, with a chop to the throat, and the accused's solicitor turned up at the dojo where I trained to find out if there were any mitigating circumstances to be found, inherent in Karate methods.

Always anxious for a story about murder, the press had a field day. Back at the K.O.A. office, we frequently took the phone off the hook, because we were choked with calls. We could not run the business and answer all the questions:

"Who was Bruce Lee?"
"Was he pure Chinese, he doesn't look it?"
"What is the best martial arts style?"
"What books did Br uce Lee write, and do you have them?"
"Who taught Bruce Lee? Can I learn from him?"
"Do you teach martial arts?"
"Where can I learn martial arts?"
"What is Kung fu? How do you spell it?"
"Is Bruce Lee really dead?"
"Who killed Bruce Lee?"
"Do you have any black belts"
"Who are you?"

Then there were the reporters who wanted anything to quote for their papers about Kung fu and Bruce Lee. It never stopped. At times, the staff of K.O.A., all four of us, thought we would go mad from phone calls. Some enterprising folks found out my home phone number and would call me in the middle of the night to ask me martial arts questions. The nightmare and the success were both down to one man - Bruce Lee. Among martial arts club owners there was a well meaning if irreverent joke, repeated more than once, to the effect that when they had said their prayers, they uttered a quiet thank you to him, and bowed in the direction of either Hong Kong or Seattle, where he was buried.

No one who did not live through that hectic period can really imagine what it was like. There have been other martial arts stars such as Jackie Chan, Claude van Damme, Chuck Norris and attempts at Bruce Lee look-a-likes, but the ripples they made cannot be compared with the storm that Lee evoked.

His wife Linda was author and co-author of several books about him, and she was gracious enough to endorse the second edition of a book which we published in 1998 called "Path to Wing Chun" by Samuel Kwok. She was grateful on Bruce Lee's behalf to the art of Wing Chun, her husband's first love in the martial arts, and said so. One can only wonder at the hand of fate which took from her not only her husband but their son Brandon Lee, himself poised at the start of a career in film.

Linda Lee not only wrote, but also helped others to put together some of Bruce Lee's writings, notes and sketches into a coherent form so that enthusiasts could at least read something of what the star thought about Jeet Kune Do.

Meanwhile, back at K.O.A. we ploughed on. Bruce Lee faded somewhat into the background, and prominent pupils of his such as Dan Inosanto, James DeMile, Richard Bustillo and others, who were already martial artists when they met him, came forward.

This book is necessarily divided up. It is derived from the K.O.A. of the time, with insertions from myself and quotations from others. It is not a biography of Lee, nor an exposition of his art, nor a critique of his films; at the same time it is in part all of these. That being said, I hope we can be forgiven if we convey any false impressions. The book is an impression from

England. A great deal has been written from the Californian point of view, and that of Hong Kong. Maybe these are more valid, more accurate, but Lee himself was not really a Californian after all, but a young Chinese who found himself famous in a foreign country, surrounded by foreigners brought up in entirely different surroundings from his own.

England, and Europe have a martial tradition of their own too, which Bruce Lee read about when he turned his attention to sword-play, and comparing it with the fundamentals of Wing Chun Kung Fu. We also have a long history of boxing, and France a tradition of kickboxing in the shape of Savate, or Boxe Francaise, not to mention wrestling in several styles throughout the whole of Europe.

The fact that we have for the last 30 or more years been on the receiving end of American, Japanese and Chinese martial arts fashions has not interrupted a solid English or British core of martial arts study. Many British martial artists have either acquitted themselves very well against foreign opposition or become champions. As I remember, we have beaten first class opponents from a very wide range of countries. This shows that in the combative as distinct from the kata-form arena we have been able to adopt foreign styles and excel at them every bit as well as the indigenous population. This is something the Brits have had to swallow in the fields of cricket, soccer and rugby football.

In kata or form competitions we have also won gold medal honours on the world stage. Therefore it is quite valid to bring forward an English view of the events of Bruce Lee's career and its aftermath.

As I have tried to indicate, the overall impact on an editor like myself of a magazine such as K.O.A. was indescribable. To give an analogy, it was like being hit by wave after wave of sea water, and in between gasping for breath amid the foam and spray. News of style after style appeared, together with experts claiming heaven knows what, accompanied by film news and championship news. To separate the wheat from the chaff was a difficult process.

Now after all this time and the sea having receded a little and

the foam dispersed, it is possible to look back with a degree of calm to speak about it.

It is interesting to try to see who is left from that period. Many people did nothing more than let themselves be pulled along in the wake of Bruce Lee, and when the pressure of interest faded, they themselves faded. Some have marched on. Others have passed away.

In the field of martial arts books, many appeared at that time. Some have remained in print, proving their intrinsic worth. Others have gone out of print, not because they contained nothing of value but because the publisher lost interest. Still more were not contributing much and disappeared when the temporary fans disappeared.

Plenty of con-men surfaced, one claiming in the early 1970's that he had made ten thousand pounds in one weekend teaching gullible students the "secrets" of martial arts. This is about sixteen and half thousand U.S. dollars. Twenty years ago of course that was worth much more than it is now.

Some of these themes are followed at more length in this book.

I do not want to give an overly critical tone about what took place in the past. But any "insider's" view is bound to have its gloom side. Some of the things which happened it would be unhelpful to put into print and harm numbers of people. This has been left out. Apologies to the sensation seekers!

I hope that the book is of interest especially to the older readers of K.O.A. who shared with me and the staff many of the events described, the attitudes taken and the thrills and enjoyment of the boom, largely initiated by Bruce Lee.

Traditionalists often criticised him, the fans loved him, and everyone in one way and another benefited from his life, and sadly from his death. What was it all about?

*****

Some Endorsement!

Dan Inosanto knows a good thing when he sees it! Here he is with Greek born George Sfetas after an Escrima and Kali stick fighting course, reading the one and only "Karate & Oriental Arts" magazine. No one knows what Dan said at the time and even fewer know what he was thinking! Thanks to Tim Ward of 'Fighters' magazine for the pic. *This picture and caption appeared in KOA no. 83 for March-April 1980. Cover stories: Simon Lau Wing Chun, Ho Bun Un Gung Lik Kune, and Toddy Sitiwatjana Thai Boxing.*

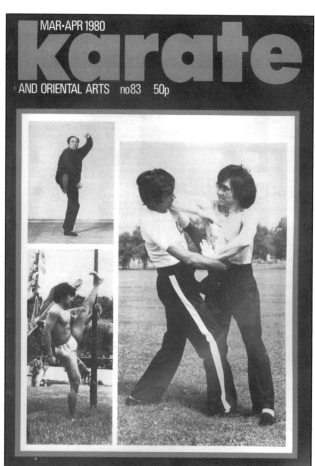

MAR·APR 1980
karate
AND ORIENTAL ARTS no83 50p

PRICES!!!

In those days KOA cost 50p. or approximately 75 cents US

nunchaku cost 3.75 ($5.62)

karate suits 11.50 ($17.25)

kung fu shoes 2.95 ($4.42)

Tao of Jeet Kune Do 6.95 ($10)

Karate-do Kyohan 8.95 ($13.42)

Bruce Lee the Man only I knew cost a remarkable 1.25 ($1.95)

and Bruce Lee's 4 volume book on his Fighting Method cost a mere 4.15 ($6.22) each

The Hong Kong published mags. such as Bruce Lee In Action cost 1.95 ($2.95)

Those were the days!

A selection of people who received training from Bruce Lee or who influenced him

Grandmaster Yip Man

Tim Tackett

Jesse Glover

Cass Magda

William Cheung

Dan Inosanto

Larry Hartsell

Richard Bustillo

James (Yimm) Lee

Bruce Lee

Chris Kent

Chuck Norris

James DeMile

James Coburn

Steve McQueen

Joe Hyams

Joe Lewis

Paul Vunak

James Garner

NOV·DEC 1980

karate

AND ORIENTAL ARTS   no 87   60p

Gung Lik Kune
Kobudo Weapons
Karate-do

In 1980 Dan Inosanto
was no longer just
holding up
a copy of K.O.A.

He was on the cover!

karate

Cover Stories

Our cover man needs no introduction to readers, apart from those who live inside a paper bag. He is no less than Dan Inosanto, who visited these shores earlier in the year and who is now willing to travel to all and any dojos in his crusade to spread the art of escrima. Part of his programme of seminars includes dips into jeet kune do and any progressions which he has made since coming into contact with a wider range of calls on his skills. If called on to do so, he can teach most of the Filipino martial arts, but as such a study would take decades, he is obliged to limit himself in his seminars to a limited range.

"I am not a master in the Filipino martial arts," he says, "just an instructor 'Guro' . . . once you have learned the basics from one instructor you must seek elsewhere. The 'elsewhere' is within yourself."

In spite of Dan's modest claim not to be a master, he is, for most people, a virtual weapons master. He was an athlete at school, a student of Ed Parker in Kenpo a little later, and when he met Bruce Lee he had already gone far into Escrima. In spite of his earlier training he found that

contact with Lee knocked him sideways, psychologically speaking. "I couldn't sleep that night," he wrote. ". . . It was something I had never seen." He went on to associate with Bruce Lee for another nine years, and as we know, to appear with him in films. He was also to initiate Bruce into the stick art of Kali which played such a powerful part in building up the 'Game Of Death' martial arts interest. Daniel Lee, Richard Bustillo and Jerry Poteet were other expert martial artists around at the time. They all gave and took from one another in those days. The tide of the 'boom' was just beginning to run, turning into a tidal wave which broke with the death of Lee and continued fall and flood all areas of martial arts activity for years to come. Since that time, Dan Inosanto has slowly developed his own swell of popularity. His style has become 'no style', which is the style that Lee himself advocated so tirelessly. But, to have 'no style' is to become a virtual master martial artist, which is what Dan claimed he is not. Meanwhile, master or not, his following grows. But even so, the chief weakness of the Filipino martial arts as a mass interest focus is that it has little in the way of cultural background interest to offer the myth-hungry western followers. Compared to Japan or China it appears to be almost destitute. Perhaps it is not Dan Inosanto's aim to build up a worldwide following for the Filipino way.

Northern Shaolin

Spinoza

Krishnamurti

Wing Chun

Tai Chi Chuan

Indian Wrestling

Western Boxing

Taekwondo

A selection of influences on Bruce Lee as found in his books, films and teaching.

Locking techniques as found in Judo,

Western Fencing

A wide variety ancient and up to the minute body training programmes

Western Wrestling

Escrima

Music, rhythm as a means of giving naturalness to martial arts

Confucianism

Taoism

Zen Buddhism

The challenge and the problem must surely have been to sort it all out?

PART ONE
FILM IMPACTS

Silent Flute

Way of the Dragon

Fist of Fury
1972

Birth of a Man

The Green Hornet (TV)

Marlowe (TV)

Game of Death
1973

Enter the Dragon
1973

The Big Boss
1971

Longstreet
(TV)

My Son A-Chang

Bruce Lee the Man and the Legend
1973

Bruce Lee starred in, appeared in, or contributed to these films

ENTER THE
DRAGON

Bruce Lee had a nickname, "Little Dragon", so perhaps it was no coincidence that his first western-backed film was called "Enter the Dragon". Until this film appeared, his fame and popularity had been limited to Hong Kong Kung fu movies and appearances on American television in supporting roles... It was a tragic twist of fate which saw to it that he was more famous after his death, than during his life.

Some twenty-five years after the appearance of this famous film, certain scenes, certain sequences and certain pieces of dialogue have stood the test of the passage of time; but the rest has not. Even during the period of its first release, the incredibly bad "Japanese Karate" sequences on the island, where massed "morons" mumbled mantras and punched in a pathetic imitation of a Karate dojo training scene, did not worry the fans. Why was a renegade Shaolin monk ruling over bands of Chinese Japanese Karate students, most of whom would not have made green belt grading?

It was part of the Chinese Kung fu movie tradition to pour scorn on all Japanese martial arts, and avenge China's treatment at the hands of Japanese occupying forces through humiliating them via the movie media. Was it a continuation of this theme in those scenes of "Enter the Dragon" referred to, where it is all one can do to stop oneself from curling up in one's seat from embarrassment as one watches, incredulously, as a martial arts based production parades such poor technique before one's very eyes?

Contrast this mass sub-mediocrity with the much better technical level of the supporting actors, such as John Saxon and Jim Kelly, and of course the star himself, Bruce Lee. The Hong Kong movie scene was not really lacking in

THE FIRST
AMERICAN PRODUCED
MARTIAL ARTS SPECTACULAR!
WITH THE LEGENDARY
BRUCE LEE

Enter The Dragon X

BRUCE LEE · JOHN SAXON · AHNA CAPRI in "ENTER THE DRAGON".
Co-Starring BOB WALL · SHIH KIEN and Introducing JIM KELLY
Music Lalo Schifrin Written by Michael Allin Produced by Fred Weintraub and Paul Heller
in association with Raymond Chow Directed by Robert Clouse
PANAVISION · TECHNICOLOR · Celebrating Warner Bros. 50th Anniversary
A Warner Communications Company
ORIGINAL SOUND TRACK ALBUM
ON WARNER BROS. RECORDS NO K46275

Just before "Enter the Dragon" was released in London, K.O.A. received a Press flyer from Edward A. Patman, in the Warner Bros. publicity and advertising department in Wardour Street, London. The informative text outlined the plot of the film, and gave thumb nail sketches of the stars.

Speaking of Bruce Lee, they credited the star with being the cause of the rise in martial arts film popularity... "his combination of physical strength, good looks and acting style made him the top martial arts star in films". Ahna Capri "first gained fame in Germany as a magazine model..."; Jim Kelly, "a handsome, sinewy black youth... karate fighter and teacher...1971 International Middle Weight Karate Champion..."; Bob Wall, "1970 United States Professional Karate Champion.."; Peter Archer, "1971 Commonwealth Karate Champion..."; Yang Sze, "Shotokan Champion of Southeast Asia..."; "Angela Mao Ying, Black Belt Hapkido Champion of Okinawa..."; "plus more than 200 other martial artists from around the world".

martial arts extras able to portray an efficient work force, suitable for Han's island cesspool where misery equals money. Were they all unfamiliar with Karate? Or was this lack of recruitment enterprise down to a common phenomenon in many action movies, where the villains attack in such an unbelievably bad way that the hero cannot help shining in contrast? Bruce Lee needed no such assistance in making his ability stand forth.

Or was the reason for hired help's bad performance that the film's producers simply wanted to present a visual experience in which the background martial arts did nothing but enhance the skills of the main protagonists? If this was the reason then they were probably mistaken in making such a choice. To show a star against a drab technical background is not a good idea. If a star is shown fighting someone who is almost as good, then when the star wins, it is an achievement. If he defeats a beginner, or rather, a martial arts fool, then what glory is there in that? If you look attentively at the film you will see that almost never does anyone attack Bruce Lee with even a half good attack. As for defence, forget it. Disappointing fight scene staging. It must have pleased people who were jealous of Lee's success.

Or was the reason for the hired help a matter of audience psychology? Did it somehow reflect the film maker's view of the fans? Did they think the fans were too ignorant to notice? Or was it simply a question of money? Or, something else? The choice, as they say, is yours.

Part of the problem in making the film was clearly the makers' difficulties in "blending" East and West themes and genres. "Enter the Dragon" in content was a kind of James Bond meets Kung Fu. The Hong Kong Kung Fu movies had always been long on action and relatively short on other things. Revenge, putting things back to rights, "Josey Wales" style and similar patterns were the motives for the action sequences, and fans thrilled to the skills and spills.

"Enter the Dragon" was intended to please audiences the world over, which as it turned out it did. Or rather, Bruce Lee did. What happened in the film was that some scenes really stood out, memorably, and others were included to hold the story together at the expense of credibility and standards.

When the martial artists arrive to take part in the tournament on Han's island there are groups of martial arts men lined up in different areas, all shouting what are supposed to be "kiai", in completely wooden postures, some badly dressed and no credit to Han at all. They are supposed to be men who candefend Han (Shek Kin), "the surrogate Dr. No", to the death, and at the very least put on a good martial arts performance. All through the film whenever they appear, they never remotely live up to this expectation. Contrast and compare this with the film which Bruce Lee intended to make himself, but which his untimely death thwarted, in which David Carradine and others starred, "The Silent Flute", also featured in this anthology. It is something of a mystery to this editor why "Enter the Dragon" fell down so badly in this respect. No criticism of Bruce Lee himself or his co-stars is intended, but if Lee's films are to be included in the annals of martial arts movies, then they must also stand up to scrutiny. The blame must lie elsewhere.

In addition to "The Silent Flute", and its proximity to Lee's creative media work, there are plenty of action films with a martial arts theme whose martial skills, philosophy and plotting show that to have martial arts does not mean that a film must sacrifice everything else. Look at some of the Jackie Chan range, the serious work of Akiro Kurosawa ("Seven Samurai", "Throne of Blood", "Sanjuro"), the landmark movie "A Touch of Zen", and others. If Bruce Lee had not been the star of the film, and the role had been taken by some unknown name, would it have even been shown more than once? Be that as it may, it is a testament to Lee's magnetic martial arts presence that the film grossed a great deal at the box office, in video sales and other media spin-offs.

Also in this anthology, we include records of the attempts which were made to "replace" Bruce Lee. He was not only poised to become perhaps one of the biggest movie stars of all time, but whichever studio had him under contract would have also been poised discover several oil wells in its film lots. It was as much a financial ploy on the part of the movie industry as it was anything else, to stage such a search for a replacement, and other lesser stars were being hauled in front of the camera as the hunger for martial arts movies grew. In the U.K., cinemas began to have special late night showings to meet the demands of fans, and magazines featuring Lee using the same old photographs over and over again appeared like magic. No one tired of seeing Bruce with the parallel cuts from Han's artificial weapon hand, cuts incidentally which did not bleed! Big pictures, cropped pictures, coloured pictures, black and white pictures, stills from films, sketches, paintings, story lines, the fans lapped them all up. In the meantime, Jackie Chan was developing his own versions of Kung fu movies, laced in the earlier days with great humour, as well as action. Needless to say, neither humour nor action nor superlative skill could substitute for Bruce Lee. He was one of a kind.

We first catch sight of our hero stripped to the waist, wearing gloves which instantly became world famous and were copied and marketed in profusion. He shows his skill in what is truly a memorable sequence, and then turns his attention to a youngster who is clearly his protege. During this scene, Lee emphasises that it is important to "feel", to use "feeling" when training. The lad is duly impressed, and Lee has sounded a note which is to ring throughout the rest of his own performance.

In every scene, Lee conveys a sense of power under control; of power which is subdued until required. In this respect it has a feline quality, which martial arts fans know is part of the range of techniques and styles of Chinese Kung fu: tiger and leopard for instance.

On the ship taking the contestants from the mainland to the island, the antipodean, reminiscently neanderthal bully who flashes a punch close to Lee's face, and asks him what is his martial arts style, is a perfect customer for the Zen-inspired trick Lee immediately plays on him. Lee says that his style is the style of fighting by not fighting. He invites the bully to row to a nearby island so that he can display the style. The bully gets into a rowing boat, and Lee pushes the boat away, retaining a hold on the line. As the bully floats into the wake of the ship, Lee "allows himself the liberty of a rare smile", (which is a quotation I have been waiting to use since I was about eight years old, from a potted biography of another loner, T.E. Lawrence). The crew grin over the stern as water laps around the bully's feet. Zen...

Arrived on the island the contestants disembark and go to their quarters. In the evening a banquet scene underlines again perhaps the scorn which the Chinese wish to pour on all things Japanese martial. Throughout the banquet, two comparatively skinny would-be Sumo wrestlers hug one another. There is no throwing from the wrestlers, no signs of martial life, except the constant hugging and pulling on their respective fundoshi! A truly memorable sight, for the wrong reasons. Who put that scene in and left it in?

When Han appears with his expert Chinese women dart throwers we are back on firm ground, and Chinese skill is displayed. Then comes the tournament... The martial skills are all acceptable and Lee in particular of course is given ample opportunity to show his control and physical development. Off camera we are treated(?) to the snap, crackle and pop of luckless contestants having their backs broken.

Lee confronts the devilish Oharra, who was instrumental in the Chinese woman's death. We know that the chips are down and we are going to see something special. We are not disappointed. Lee performs his now legendary back flip kick, describing a circling backwards somersault at the same time kicking Ohara in the face. This technique, though repeated in other martial arts films, was more or less a new sight for western fans, and when "Enter the Dragon" appeared on video must have been re-run countless times. Once defeated, Oharra breaks the code and attacks Lee with two broken glass bottles. Lee demolishes him. Han is not pleased.

Espionage fits Lee like a glove, and he slips cat-like through his mission, doing away with guards like autumn leaves in the wind. In her book about him, Linda Lee reported that he was actually bitten by the cobra in rehearsal; fortunately the snake had had its venom removed. We get to see John Saxon in action, and Jim Kelly, both giving creditable and credible performances. Then to the showdown, the long sequence culminating in the hall of mirrors scene with Han. This contest is full of interesting impressions, and like other scenes merits more than one viewing to get the full taste of it. To begin with, Han is obviously someone with martial arts training, in real life, not simply according to the plot. He looks capable, he looks dangerous, he looks confident. When he sizes Lee up during the contest you can see the measured look of a martial artist, and when he attacks it is with decision and knowledge of what he is about. If we did not know that Lee is the hero and that he is bound to win in the end, we might back Han as the winner, helped by his artificial "knife hands".

Han's sudden death comes not from a superior martial technique from Lee but a piece of good timing, and even luck for Lee. From this point of view, though we feel Han has got his just reward, being impaled on one of his own collection of weapons, it might have been more satisfactory if Lee had beaten him after one last, fiery exchange of blows that showed up the star's superior skill. As it is, Lee is badly if theatrically scarred, and departs with a question mark hanging over them both; was Lee the better martial artist? Some critics have dubbed this final scene a type of narcissist exercise for Lee, where he could display his own physique and admire it himself as he played with death. We know that he was pre-occupied with his own bodily development and always trying to test himself to the limits of speed and muscle coordination, but it seems to me that the scene is merely the climax of a series of contests and punch-ups. The setting, a museum of death followed by a confusing hall of mirrors, adds menace and uncertainty to the outcome in a way that a combat in an ordinary room or beach or garden would certainly not have done. Will one of Han's weapons collections finish Lee off? Will Lee be injured by smashing glass? Will Lee himself pick up one of the weapons and teach Han how to use it? None of these. Lee relies upon his empty hands and feet, enduring the pain from the steel blades, pursuing the face of evil to the bitter end.

We are made to suffer the suspense as each image in the mirrors turns out to be a false one, give a little cheer inside as the hero decides to smash each mirror to prevent it from giving a deceptively real reflection, and wait hopefully for the final blow, asking if Han will stay down this time. When he is finally impaled on the revolving door, there is a tinge of irony at the thought that the villain dies seeing the chief regions of his domain spinning before his darkening eyes.

For me, Han is barely second to Lee in his martial presence and cinematic charisma. In some ways, for instance in the wealth of age and experience which comes through the boundaries of his role and lines, it might be argued that he does overshadow Lee. Lee was by comparison new to acting, in the sense of being able to convey a sense of power without recourse to any martial implications, whilst Han was a man with an acting past, and it showed.

Seeing "Enter the Dragon" again in 1998 it was a clear example to me of a production which shows its age. It is memorable only because it is one of the few examples of Bruce Lee on film. It is memorable because we see the star in action, albeit with the constraints of the film makers. But Lee apart it is not memorable for the other martial arts sequences, the "acting" of the extras, the dialogue, apart from a few choice pearls from the star, the wardrobe or anything else. It has been surpassed many times in these respects by other martial arts movies.

It is certain that had Bruce Lee lived, he would have gone on to make independent films where he would have had a free hand, been guided by friends and film stars like James Coburn, and writers like Joe Hyams. In the next chapter we look at "The Silent Flute", which would have been a project such as this, with Lee in the leading role. This was fundamentally a jewel of an idea for a martial arts movie. It had the powerful element of a mysterious quest for some kind of philosophical truth or personal understanding and in a sense would have been a portrayal of Lee's own search for martial arts perfection, a perfection which he had sought on the individual level, and a perfection he could have tried to share with his fans on the silver screen. Different writers have pointed out that the budgets for Hong Kong movies, the type Lee had starred in and seen, were very small compared with those of Hollywood. It was not quite shoe-string, but Linda Lee reminds us for instance that the glass used in the Hollywood movies is some type of harmless sugary material, but in Hong Kong they just used real glass, to save money!

What always interested me, and something which I found out more about when K.O.A. began to make video programmes, was the enormous difference between what happens during the making of a film and what the movie-goer sees on the screen. As we got more and more into video I began to watch films in a different way, and saw how the camera angles were changing, how the distance was changing, how cuts were made and why. Sometimes cuts are introduced by the censor, and it shows; at other times you can see how the editor or director has timed a cut amazingly well, sometimes cutting from a scene which is very well picked up in the next, or as it were opening a new chapter in the story by a cut which brings a totally new atmosphere to it. There are changes of pace, colour, music, mood, and this is all constructed from what are virtually pieces of moving jigsaw. In some respects, cutting and editing is more interesting than filming. Bruce Lee's fighting sequences are an enormous challenge to any editor, provided he is given sufficient material by the director or the producers. Apparently there was a great deal of Bruce on film which was simply scrapped. Someone, some time later, must have been kicking himself for that...

In these respects the editing on the boat scenes was very good, particularly the brief scene with the martial arts bully. The banquet was not. The early scene in which the Chinese young woman is chased and eventually killed was pure Hong Kong Kung Fu Movie. One aspect of this was the enormous amount of punishment the antagonists take before they eventually go down and stay down. People can have chairs smashed on them, men can be kicked in the testicles, fall down stairs, and get all manner of terrible things done to them and they fight on, or they run after someone else. In contrast the tournament scene showed people being hit, going down, and staying down. In my own experience this is more true to life, but is a martial arts movie meant to be true to life? The Hong Kong fans wanted a battle royal and in the pursuit of the woman they got it. The editor got his material and knew the formula. It is an interesting exercise to look at "Enter the Dragon" in the ways briefly mentioned above. You should also bear in mind the role of the continuity person, who has to make sure that if for instance Bruce Lee's scratch marks are so many inches or centimetres long and begin and end at a certain point in his body, on Friday's shoot, then if he re-appears for some more takes on Monday then they are in exactly the same place. If they are longer or have moved, some twelve year old schoolboy fan will see this and let everybody know. The same thing applies to scenery, and camera positions. Fallen, broken chairs must be in the same place, bandages must be in the same place and not on the opposite leg. The same with dents in crashed cars, and so on, and on. If the continuity person does not work efficiently, the jigsaw will not fit together and there will be endless glitches of vision which observant audiences will pick up, leaving a taste of unprofessional work in the mouths of their eyes!

So all these factors, and more, have to fit into one continuous experience for the audience. It is a big challenge. In addition to these common factors, Hong Kong has others. It is such a noisy city that films are shot without sound, because it is impossible to exclude extraneous sound. This means that films have to have all sound dubbed on to the soundtrack afterwards. Of course dubbing goes on in most films. It is in itself a big discipline for the dubbing editors, and for the actors, if they are to produce a credible result. If you have ever seen a foreign movie with English dubbed on to it, when you watch the actors speaking you can see that they are not speaking English, but you accept it. If this were to occur in an English speaking film it would be laughable, however serious the theme. Part of Bruce Lee's work after the making of "Enter the Dragon" was to produce sound for the dubs. He felt very responsible towards the standard of the finished product, and this part of the construction must have been a strain in itself, in addition to all the other currents which were running through his life at the time. James Coburn, so Linda Lee reported, felt that the star felt under tremendous strain and threat. He did not know whom to trust. It was part of his dual role: film star and seeker for martial arts perfection. If you add to that the role of businessman, father, husband, teacher, Chinese in what was more and more an American setting, it was understandable.

What really passed through the star's mind as he saw "Enter the Dragon" take shape?

K.O.A. 1985/6

MARTIAL ARTS YEARBOOK

William Cheung's Death Touch — Cheng's Tai Chi — Hong Kong Police Training — Shadows of Iga Festival — Taekwondo — Wadoryu Karate — Judo — Japanese Sword — Thai Boxing — Aiki Techniques — Frank Dux — Chinese & Japanese Weapons, and more . . .

£2.50

K.O.A. featured Wing Chun patriarch Yip Chun, teacher and friend of Samuel Kwok. Briefly we covered the famous Jujutsu instructor Professor Wally Jay, his Small Circle theory and relevance to Bruce Lee. The article read:

Professor Jay has long been an innovator of new techniques and counts among his friends... Nils Erik Loustad (Norway), Don Jacobs (Trinidad), Ronald Forrester (Canada), Ed Parker, and the most famous of all, Bruce Lee. Both Bruce and Wally were non-classical martial artists; indeed it was Professor Jay who wrote the introduction to Bruce Lee's first book, "Chinese Gung Fu - Philosophical Art of Self Defense" in 1963. Many ideas were exchanged by these two great martial artists; neither wholly agreed on patterns (kata), both agreed in going all out when performing techniques, both believed strongly in wrist action; this can be seen in Bruce's famous 3" punch, which... may have been developed after discussions with Profesor Jay....

Sam Allred... instrumental in the writing of Bruce Lee Memorial Book, states: "Perhaps the most valid means of sharing my feelings about Wally in the fewest words would be to share my knowledge of Bruce Lee's praise for him. He (Bruce) seriously studied Wally's techniques and teaching methods and he had an active and sincere interest in Wally's various martial arts projects. Bruce was proud to count him among his few really trusted friends".

Chris Casey states: "Bruce Lee's star status is the result of being in the right place at the right time and having the sense to recognise you, (Wally Jay) as the final authority on martial arts."

The
Silent Flute
(The Film Bruce Lee wished to make)

David Carradine in "The Silent Flute" ("The Circle of Iron") plays a flute which he made himself. He was unhappy about most aspects of the film and said so.

Cord takes on the Monkey Man, Jungar, one of David Carradine's metamorphoses.

Many film stars must think of writing and producing a film some day, and many have. Bruce Lee was one of those and "The Silent Flute" (a.k.a. "The Circle of Iron") was the name of his hoped for production. Fate intervened and it was left to his friends, pupils and the movie business to fulfil his ambition for him. The result was an enjoyable martial arts movie with the theme of a quest, or search, probably Lee's own search. Star David Carradine thought it could have been a lot better...

The American magazine "Martial Arts Movies" interviewed David Carradine in its 1982 January issue about the film and about Kung fu on the screen. Carradine made a very good point about the latter. (I think it is a very good point because it agrees with what I think!) The point was that in many action scenes you do not really see what is going on. Carradine said,

> "In 'Enter the Dragon' a stuntman comes in and does a somersault over the heads of the people and you think it's Bruce."

He said that he was against Kung fu sequences which were not based on clear, candid renditions of what was actually going on.

> "I believe the best martial arts film would be a simple rendition, with good camera work, good direction, of what it is that happens to a man's body when he's doing kung fu."

He said that he was disappointed in the "Silent Flute" and believed that if the script had been written by really excellent writers then both he and Jeff Cooper who plays the main character Cord "could have been brought to great heights". Apparently whilst Carradine was looking to get the film production moving another company bought the original rights. The principal man involved, Sandy Howard, maker of "A Man Called Horse", wanted Carradine to play the lead but he refused. The overall impression from the interview is that the star was very unhappy about the way in which the film had been made and considered that the opportunity to produce a truly memorable picture had been thrown away. It showed us that we, Joe Public, just don't know what goes on, and that considerations of martial arts values some-times come very low on the list of priorities.

When K.O.A. began to make martial arts instructional videos, one of them was on Jujutsu. I knew nothing about video making when we began but I had been con-stantly there whilst recording (filming) was in progress and I knew what I wanted the viewer to see. The Jujutsu tape was our fourth subject. Towards the end of the programme there is a scene where several Jujutsu students are all fighting at once.

As David Carradine said, I too wanted the scene to be clear to the viewer, mainly because the tape was instructional; it was obvious. In the midst of the recording, we got some shots which were close-up, fuzzy, confusing, where only parts of the students' bodies were visible. When we came to view and edit the whole sequence, the camera men and the professional editor applauded these fuzzy, indistinct scenes. I had to get to the bottom of their enthusiasm and understand it.

I could see that if the programme had been a story, a feature film, then the indistinct scenes could have provided an element of suspense, to make the audience wonder how the fight would turn out, and so forth. But this was not a feature film but a teaching programme. We had a mild argument about it and in the end I agreed to keep the scene in the final edit. I had already played this scene(!) during the making of our first effort which dealt with White Crane Kung Fu featur-ing the excellent English martial artist Bob Stannells. In the editing room of Sony in West London I had virtually had a verbal stand up fight with the director and editor about the very same point. Slowly as we continued to make video tapes like this I got the message that there were certain conventions, currently in vogue, and all the professionals expected these conventions to be followed, irrespective of the subject or the aims of the makers. It puzzled me, and I did not for the most part let these conventions dictate what we did.

In the event our productions were well received by the martial arts world and eventually found distribution in the United States as well as Europe. As a footnote to David Carradine's comments on the use of a stuntman in "Enter the Dragon", readers may not know that very frequently film companies insist that the stars of films do not endanger themselves during the making of a movie as this would hold up the production and cost a great deal of cash. This was probably the cogent reason in this instance; not that Lee could not do his own stunts!

At the Pingree Studios on Sunset Boulevard, Los Angeles, the news of the coming film "Silent Flute" was announced, and "Black Belt" magazine was the one to announce it to the martial arts world. Film star James Coburn (Cross of Iron, In Like Flint, Magnificent Seven), Stirling Silliphant (Academy award winner for screen play in "In the Heat of the Night") and Bruce Lee himself got together to put the story and script into some kind of shape. Bruce Lee said that "Stirling and Jim are doing the martial arts the greatest credit ever." James Coburn explained that, "Thearts are used as a tool to portray the self-evolution of a man. Martial arts then really becomes a means to an end."

Stirling Silliphant praised Coburn's personal qualities, not only as an actor but also as a student of eastern philosophy which he was trying to integrate into his own life style. He commented: "He (Coburn) doesn't just read books." Silliphant himself remained fully western in his approach to life but said that he studied Jeet Kune Do for reasons other than being able to defend himself on a dark night against muggers.

In the script writing stage of the film, when the ideas and conversation were flowing, and the harsh practicalities were perhaps on the back burner, a very idealistic "package", if there can be such a thing, was floated. The very best available martial artists were to be used for the fight scenes; men from different styles, each showing his own best, characteristic techniques, and the hero, in defeating them would to some extent be an exemplar of JKD philosophy. That is, a fixed style, a "frozen" technical series of moves, could never ultimately defeat the alive, truly spontaneous individual. At the same time, the hero himself would undergo changes, because each time he defeated another adversary... And so the thoughts about the plot flowed on. Then it was decided that to "warm up" the public, there would also be a type of documentary film released probably on television to show what martial arts were really all about. These were great thoughts, great plans, and they all made sense. But fate had other ideas.

It is not often, is it, that the best gets up on to the screen. The fashion for "serial killer" movies lasted for some years, and still trails on. "Silence of the Lambs" was hailed as the greatest by the hypers and Hollywood. But for me, the best ever film of this type was "Manhunter" played by less well known actors. As far as I am concerned, "Silence of the Lambs" was just a series of set pieces, hammed up by all the actors. If you compare it with the "Manhunter" film, you can see this very clearly. What Lee, Coburn and Silliphant wanted was, by the nature of ninety per cent of film production company habits, something which would never see the light of day. It was too good, too right and too un-Hollywood. It should have been given to Kurosawa.

Before "The Silent Flute was released in England, as editor of K.O.A. magazine, I was invited, along with numbers of other martial arts students and officials of the day, to a private view of the film in a small cinema in London's Soho, centre of show business, red lights and only a stone's throw away from Chinatown. We had been invited because the distributors wanted to know what we, as experts(?), thought of it, and would it be successful, and so forth. We took our seats. What follows is an account of what we saw.

The film can be taken at more than one level. On the face of it about one man's quest and the difficulties, and hazards of combat he must face, but below the surface it can readily be seen as a series of psychological encounters with aspects of the man's inner world which he must confront and struggle with if he is to succeed. This second level surely points towards Lee's own preoccupation with physical fitness, martial skill, and very much, as we know from accounts published, with the limitations which all human beings have eventually to recognise. In the words of another screen legend, Clint Eastwood...

"A man's got to know his limitations."

If you should ever see the picture, or have already seen it, it is worth while bearing in mind David Carradine's comments, Lee, Coburn and Silliphant's ideas, and comparing them with what you see.

(Photographs of "Silent Flute" by kind permission of Carlton International Media Ltd.)

BRUCE'S HEIRS SAW THE FULFILMENT OF HIS DREAM

James Coburn, who was a friend, pupil and colleague of Bruce Lee, co-operated with him over the original idea and story of "Silent Flute". The skill of the former was illustrated in 1967/68 in the film "In Like Flint", reviewed in "Karate & Oriental Arts" magazine No.7. His own down-toearth approach marked him out as a brother-inspirit of Cord. What is the value of fine martial arts "dancing" if the end result, self-defence, is not served? Cord storms out of the amphitheatre, vowing to conquer Zetan and learn the secrets of the Book. The whole feeling in the amphitheatre conjured up by costume designer Lilly Fenichel is a blend of Persia, China and top level Science Fantasy comixl Thoroughly enjoyable and very fascinating. The more the audience knows about martial arts in general and about Bruce Lee, the more they can enjoy and appreciate it.

The Quest Begins

Morthond sets out and realises that Cord is following him. Although he has taken a vow of silence, the Dancer breaks it and asks Cord to stop. Whilst this exchange is taking place the Blind Man walks by, with his staff, and goes into a ruined castle. Suddenly, there is an uproar. Cord charges into the ruins and beholds the Blind Man battling with a gang of six ruffians, using his staff as a weapon. David Carradine, for it is he, smashes about him left, right, up, down, round, and rapidly despatches them all, only to vanish as inexplicably as he arrived. Cord can hardly believe the exhibition of skill he has witnessed. He is impressed more than he can say. The blind man's fight from a combination of hearing and what kung-fu masters would call "hearing energy", could carefully be developed by spe-

cial training and assiduous practise. This is a figure traditionally appearing in martial arts stories and sagas. It also underlines the fact that in real life some of the greatest masters suffered from some infirmity which led them to extra efforts to overcome it. These extra efforts made them into the great masters they were. The implication is that the Blind Man's lack of sight made it necessary for him to become supremely sensitive.

Monkey...

Time has elapsed; Cord continues his journey, when suddenly he sees Morthond the Dancer who went on ahead. He is fatally injured. What has happened? Evidently someone else has outwitted Morthond's technique. Cord hears the screeches of a band of monkey-like men. The Dancer bemoans his failure in The First Trial. He proffers the Medallion of the quest to Cord, and dies. The First Trial faces Cord now, and he squares up to Jungar, the Monkey Man, played by David Carradine. To an orchestra of discordant monkey screams and yells in a cave-like hall, illuminated by scattered, flickering fires, Jungar attacks. Cord receives the full fury of the animalpowered monkey techniques. He is afraid, bewildered by the inhuman speed of his attacker. But, steadily recalling the skill of the Blind Man, he counters and wears Jungar down into defeat. As Monkey style is a style of Kung fu, (illustrated from "Inside Kung Fu" magazine), this sequence is perhaps an indication that the No-Style of Cord is more than a match for the animal monkey tradition. Cord continues on his way, shaken but victorious. In the distance he can hear a flute. The Blind Man is not far away.

He enters a desert and as he crosses he comes upon a man who is standing in a barrel of oil. This Man In Oil is trying to dissolve his sexual powers and so rid himself of temptations of the flesh. This is probably a poke(!) at some of the misinterpretations of oriental yogic systems which creep into martial arts, and the audiences react with appropriate glee when this scene is played. Cord fails to be impressed by the Man In Oil's suggestion that he too should dissolve his manhood away, and bids him good morning !

Cord has taken a vow of chastity whilst on the Quest and his next encounter is to test this. He comes upon an encampment in the middle of the desert and hears the all pervading sound of music. The place is full of exotically clad men and women. Cord meets Changsha The Rhythm Man (David Carradine), who is a Turk. It is his encampment; the people serve him. Cord tries to question Changsha but gets nowhere. Cord is tested at the encampment, entertained and wooed; but he is given no answers. "Is this really the second Trial?" "Perhaps", comes the reply.

Changsha has been married many times; he offers Cord his ninth wife Tara, a dark haired beauty with glowing skin and gleaming eyes. Cord refuses Tara, and retires for the night. Tara comes to him again. His young flesh is too strong for him, and he sweetly succumbs to her call. He falls deeply in love with her, and asks her to share his life, his love and his quest. They fall into a deep sleep.

Cord awakens the following day. He is alone. All have gone. The desert is empty except for one appalling sight: Tara-crucified. Now, Cord is overcome with grief. He staggers on in quest of Zetan, but his heart is not in it. Eventually he comes upon another ruined fortress. He is stalked by the Pantherman (David Carradine). In keeping with his dark skin the Pantherman is attacking at night, but somehow Cord is able to shake off his sorrow and fight back with surprising force and skill. Perhaps Pantherman is the incarnation of Death, come too soon, for Cord drives him away, and at that moment hears the soothing sound of the flute once more.

Blind Man's Help

We sense the Blind Man is somehow more open towards Cord than at the beginning of the story. Cord asks him if he can accompany him. The Blind Man agrees, but makes the condition that Cord must ask him nothing until such time as he, in his own time, shall agree to it. Their quiet journey is shattered as horsemen bear down on them. Men clad in a strange mediaeval mixture of clothing sweep into the attack. Cord throws his sharp, starred shuriken to deadly effect. The Blind Man uses his bamboo staff once again. Together they destroy the new threat. All at once, drums draw Cord to the seashore. He encounters Changsha's caravan once more. This time Cord is to fight the Turk. Comes the dawn. Changsha changes as the fight progresses, but Cord see through one ruse after another. He pursues the Turk relentlessly, perhaps helped by the memory of the cruelly murdered Tara. At length Changsha is defeated. It is the final trial. Cord receives his answer: "The way is across the water."

Seeing Himself

Cord makes the journey across the water and is shown into the grounds of a mediaeval monastery. The scent of flowers fills the air; the setting seems wrong for combat. It is. Cord is led into the presence of Zetan (Christopher Lee). The young man has failed to "tune" himself to the atmosphere of the monastery. "When do we fight?" he asks. Zetan ignores the question and tells Cord that he must rehearse a ceremony, the ceremony which inducts him into Keepership of the Book of Enlightenment. Cord is filled with confusion. Eventually the Book is handed to him. Cord takes it, aware that it may be more of a trial than all his other trials put together. He opens the first page. He finds that he is looking into a mirror. He turns the next page- a mirror. Each page shows him his own face. The scene fades inexplicably, showing Cord travelling once again. Once more he meets the Blind man, to the sound of a flute. The Blind Man asks him what he saw. "Everything!" Cord exclaims.

Trying very hard
to look like **Bruce Lee...**

But not really succeeding...

With Bruce Lee gone, one not totally unexpected development was the staging of a contest to see if anyone resembling him could be found. A further notion was to find(?) an actor with a similar name such as Bruce Li, Bruce K. L. Lea and yet another one called Bruce Ly. The name Lee became very popular among Chinese movie "stars". No one really thought a replacement could be found but the moves stimulated the flow of cash.

Attempts were also made to re-invent his life; biography would be too strong a word. It goes without saying that some of these efforts were viewed with a certain degree of scepticism by many martial artists, but in defence of such efforts one only has to remember that Bruce Lee was a media figure, a star, as well as a martial artist. As such he was just as much fair game as any other star.

Film-alikes appeared. "Fist of Fury 2" and "Enter the Ninja" were two, and "Dragon" became a much used word in Kung Fu movies. Bruce, Lee, Li, Dragon, Enter, Dragon, Way, Death - all words associated with the star were up for grabs; anything to associate the new film with the memory of the old.

Elvis Presley suffered a similar and more prolonged fate of a media circus after his death, and lookalike contests persist in profusion. Stars are up there and take the rough with the smooth, alive or dead. It is the price of fame, as the old saying goes. Customers visit ing the K.O.A. shop would bring up the subject of a Bruce Lee lookalike and their tones of voice would be tinged with doubt accompanied by a sort of forlorn hope that perhaps someone would come along who would fit the bill; some Bruce Lee reincarnation, some doppelganger, alive, pulsating with the same energy. Hope springs eternal in the savage breast. But it was not to be. All the fans had were what Bruce Lee had left behind. Occasionally a previously unpublished photograph would appear and the embers would flicker, and then subside.

Bruce Lee's first efforts to start his own school had taken place in Seattle. As far as he was concerned these were unsuccessful, and it was only when he moved to California that things changed. And it was in California that the search for a new Bruce Lee began in

Some five hundred young people turned up outside Stage One at the Burbank studios when Warner Bros. and First Artists held auditions for someone to portray Bruce Lee in "Bruce Lee, His Life and Legend", based on Linda Lee's book.

Significantly, the poster's image of Bruce Lee shows the face blank, waiting to be filled. It was never really filled.

Photographs courtesy of Rex Features.

earnest, in Hollywood, the land of dreams. The dollar had spoken and across the sea they had heard its voice loud and clear. "Enter the Dragon" had been Hollywood's first real taste of dealing with a Chinese martial artist as a star, and Kung Fu as a subject. It showed. The film was weak in many ways and had Bruce Lee lived the making of his future American epics would have surely been very different.

As it was, in the United States they realised that the search was futile. In Hong Kong they ploughed on, paying little or no attention to the type of considerations which rule among major Hollywood producers. The two centres were literally and figuratively miles apart. What was need-ed was a new star with his own credibility, his own style, his own pace, who would not exactly replace Lee, but fit the bill for the thirsty Kung Fu film fans.

This new star was of course Jackie Chan. Chunkily built, compared with Bruce Lee, funny, accepting all kinds of roles, moods, settings and cos-tumes, the new man on the block, as far as western audiences were con-cerned, was loved by all. Curtis F. Wong Enterprises, publishers of "Inside Kung Fu" and "Martial Arts Movies" magazines produced a thick edition of a magazine mainly focussing on Jackie Chan. It was very pop-ular. They had previously published the world famous "Bruce Lee: Untold Story" packed with photographs of Bruce Lee and people related to him or connected with him, and the Chan publication took its place alongside this. But not for long. Somehow, the magic that was Lee was not transferable.

Jackie Chan, as we all know, branched out into films which were not exactly Kung Fu, and went his own way. Martial artists such as Chuck Norris and Claude Van Damme cut their own niche, and the former Aikido expert Steve Segal made a terrific first impact with his film Nico, but he too left the martial arts on the sidelines and became an action hero. Angela Mao was well known through her film "When Taekwondo Strikes" and also in "Stoner" with George Lazenby. Carter Wong played in the same Taekwondo film with Angela Mao and the famous martial artist Jhoon Rhee showed off his own Korean martial arts alongside them. "Beach of the War Gods" and "One Armed Boxer" showed the talents of Wang Yu, and producers made sure the women were not left out of the running with their explicitly titled "Kung Fu Girl" starring Cheng Pei Pei.

Much later came the successful "Karate Kid" and its sequels, appealing directly by title and content to a much younger audience, but the young adults enjoyed it just as much. The resident elderly sifu or sensei (teacher) was always in attendance, ensuring that the protege would do the right thing. Gradually the Kung Fu movie became better and better in the spectacular sense. Fighting scenes and visual effects grew in duration and sophistication. But, no one was ever really like Bruce Lee...

Dragon, Bruce, Lee, Enter, Game, Death, Fist, Fury... were all words to conjure with... and a lot of rabbits came out of the hat...

A well known flying kick by Bruce Lee is the background for Jon Peters, co-producer, Linda Lee, Chuck Norris, Barbra Streisand and Robert Clouse, the proposed writer and director of "Bruce Lee, His Life and Legend", as they attend the talent audition for someone to portray the star, held at Stage One, the Burbank Studios. The audition was promoted by Warner Bros. and First Artists.

During the late 1970's martial arts movies declined in popularity, but by the beginning of the next decade they were climbing again. "Rip-off" and "exploitation" movies, as they were "dubbed" in the United States, based in some way on fragments of Bruce Lee's legacy, had proliferated in this period. Among the Chinese actors involved in these types of movie were Ho Tsung-tao, Dragon Lee (Bruce Lei), Kim Tai-chung and Huan Kin-lung. Film titles of this self perpetuating Bruce Lee memorabilia genre included "Game of Death 2", "Enter the Fat Dragon", "The Dragon Lives Again", "Bruce Le's Greatest Revenge", "Bruce Lee the Invincible" and "Bruce and Shaolin Kung Fu", to name but...

In "New Fist of Fury" and "Fist of Fury Part 2" the very name of the original Bruce Lee film is used quite blatantly, with some of the actors from that film taking on their old roles in "New Fist..." The movie "Enter the Fat Dragon" has been elevated from the "rip-off" plane by at least one commentator and referred to as a satire. Among the many episodes of this humorous yarn is one in which the hero goes to hell to meet James Bond, Popeye, Emanuelle, the Godfather and other heterogeneous characters. The plot must have been invented by someone who was heartily fed up with the whole post Bruce Lee scene and in consequence let his fertile imagination run wild. Perhaps it sent a message to the fans.

In 1985 a list of over thirty films in the categories we are talking about was made, and this was a a selected list. Who knows how many there are at the beginning of 1999!

"Investigative" films which "revealed" the "truth" about Bruce Lee's romantic involvements somehow belong in the pits of the pits of our film categories. Betty Ting Pei, in whose flat Lee died, was the focus of one such epic of detective work. It is no secret that the actress regretted taking part in "I Love You Bruce Lee", released about two years after his death, because the producers had changed the film content from what she had wanted, after she had unwisely handed over control to them. In the United States the title was given the more titillating title, "Bruce Lee: His Last Days (His Last Nights)".

Other combinations, permutations, edits of glued together, phantasmagoric collages of Bruce Lee scenes, imitator scenes, and fact based on fiction stories exist, of interest to only the really dedicated film buff who wants to identify every second of their confusing content. This would be real detective work. One canot help thinking that if some of the makers of these raggedy patchwork quilts had put as much effort into making a completely new, good movie as they did into collecting and assembling and editing many thousands of feet of film from all over the place they might even have come up with something to be proud of. As it was they ploughed on regardless, or as we say in Britain, "Carry on Regardless..."

in the

shape

of

copycat

films...

actors

called

'Bruce'

appeared

from

nowhere.

Names of some films which in one way or another are connected with Bruce Lee.

We had to draw the line somewhere and the list is a selection only.

Big Boss Part 2
Black Dragon versus Yellow Tiger
Bloody Hero
Bolo
Bruce and Dragon Fist
Bruce and Shaolin Bronzemen
Brucefinger
Bruce Lee, The Man and the Myth
Bruce Lee the Invincible
Bruce Lee's Secret
Bruce Lee, Super Dragon
Bruce Lee Fights Back from the Grave
Bruce Lee and I
Bruce Lee's Greatest Revenge
Bruce in New Guinea
Bruce King of Kung Fu
Bruce and Shaolin Kung Fu
Bruce and the Iron Finger
Clones of Bruce Lee
Cobra
Dragon Dies Hard
Dragon Lives
Dragon the Hero
Dragon Lives Again
Eagle King
Enter the Fat Dragon
Enter the Game of Death
Exit the Dragon, Enter the Tiger
Fear of Fear - Touch of Death
Fierce One
Fighting Dragon
Fist of Fury Part 2
Furious
Game of Death Part 2
Goodbye Bruce Lee

I Love you Bruce Lee
Image of Bruce Lee
Jeet Kune Do, the Claws and Supreme Kung Fu
Last Days of Bruce Lee
Life and Legend of Bruce Lee
New Fist of Fury
Real Bruce Lee
Return of Bruce
Return of Red Tiger
Return of the Dragon
Return of the Fist of Fury
Return of the Tiger
Seven Blows of the Dragon
Seven Men of Kung Fu
Superdragon Against Superman
Tiger Boxer
True Game of Death

This list is published only as an indication of the lengths to which film makers went to utilise the words associated either with the name of Bruce Lee or with the names of his films. It is not meant as a recommendation to view any of them or to praise or adversely criticise their content.

"Enter the Game of Death" clearly utilises words from two of his films in one title. "Fat" in "Enter the Fat Dragon" implies the subject is not going to be treated seriously.

Titles such as "Big Boss Part 2" indicate a sequel, and so on. The titles chosen are simple and direct, using as many angles as spring to mind. They play quite shamelessly on the hopes and feelings of the fans, and have been called "exploitation" films, which in the same simple sense they are.

Bruce Li was one of the more convincing lookalikes of Bruce Lee. He starred in the film "Bruce Lee, the Man, the Myth" directed by Ng See Yuen. Once you become used to the new face, which is not so very different from Lee's, at least on the screen, you see and appreciate that Li has done some work on studying the superstar's expressions, techniques of martial arts, postures, and characteristic movements.

The way Lee had of hunching forward, moving sideways when sizing up his opponent, and his lightning punches, are commendably reproduced by the screen "double". In addition, the director and Li saw to it that far more definite credit was afforded to Wing Chun both in actual content of scene and dialogue, and in the fight scenes. Techniques reminiscent of Wooden Dummy training, tan sau, lap sau and so forth can be clearly seen, and this must have been a source of satisfaction to many people. In this respect, we can hazard a guess that Bruce Lee himself might have been happy to see much of the combat in the picture.

The story begins more or less with Li meeting Grandmaster Yip Man in the latter's kwoon in Hong Kong. Disconsolate because he is leaving for America, Li tries out a few techniques on the Mak Jhong, Wooden Dummy, and then Yip Man enters, played by an actor who passes very well for the great one. They spar together for one last time, and rather over-zealously cut from the scene as Li is driving Yip Man back, forcing him to retreat. Over-zealously because it is unlikely that Li or Lee could ever have driven Yip Man back. Anyway, this is one more feather in Li's cap.

Arrived in the United States, Li is shown already impressing people with his coin-snatching skills and teaching Jeet Kune Do. The film doesn't pay a great deal of heed to chronology or importance of events in Lee's life. For example one day he is single and the next day he is married. The how, the when and the why are just not addressed at all. Linda is portrayed, if that's the word, as a piece of talking wallpaper, the repeated pattern of a "good little woman". His two sons appear from nowhere, and his paternal instincts summed up by the fact that he says "goodnight" to them.

Rather too much is made of a sneering attitude in Li to all foreign things and people. Karate is given a very bad press indeed, and Englishmen shown as loud mouthed unfit louts no doubt as payment for our behaviour at the siege of Peking and other major misdemeanours. Much is made of Lee's renowned ability to concentrate on more than one thing at a time, for instance in his contest with the Hong Kong Hung Gar(?) expert. As his opponent warms up and goes through the movements of his style, Li chats with his friend about the fight scenes in a forthcoming movie as though the coming battle did not exist.

A clear point is made about the extent to which Bruce Lee was pre-occupied with his own physical fitness and development. Arrays of modern weight training equipment and special punch testing devices are shown in one prolonged scene. Li suffers some type of traumatic episode as he trains, shrugs it off, and continues. The actor has an excellent physique and it must be admitted does credit to his part in this and other ways.

An old score and a scene "borrowing" appear in the picture too. Years previously, a team of Kung Fu men had taken on a team of Thai boxers, and suffered a humiliating defeat. Kung Fu supporters protested that the Kung Fu team had not been the most representative of the arts and were not professionals. In spite of their protestations, the defeat smarted and smouldered on in the memory. In our film, Li takes on a trio of Thai boxers in the grounds of an old temple, and defeats them all. Their leader is bound to admit the superiority of Kung Fu! The arts are vindicated at last.

In the very same scene, so that we presumably know that there is no doubt that it is Bruce Lee putting things right by Kung Fu, the wonderful shots from "Enter the Dragon" are reproduced where Lee does a backward somersault in the form of a kick to Oharra's face. Li does a very similar kick to the face of one of the Thai boxers. At the time, circles and spheres were a preoccupation of martial artists, making a distinction between them and the largely linear techniques of Japanese Karate. The similarity to the stomach throw or "tomoe-nage" of Judo to this move was what struck me at the time and we featured it in K.O.A.

Some old scores were settled on film and Chinese Kung Fu vindicated.

A striking difference between this film and its fight sequences is the number of times Li is shown in longshot, so that the audience can see clearly what he is doing. This contrasts for instance to some of the scenes in Bruce Lee's own films where long shots are not used, either for reasons of generating excitement or because of the shortcomings of the martial skills of the protagonists, that is, Lee's opponents. As David Carradine is quoted elsewhere, if you go to see a martial arts film you want to see martial art, not have it obscured by editorial preferences. This is a big plus in the film and one which was taken up by the makers of Jackie Chan films for instance. Generally, Chan's skills are shown to the full and appreciated.

Some latitude is used to show Bruce Lee defeating a number of challengers and the event at Ed Parker's Long Beach tournament is somewhat confusing. As Li eventually is successful on television and in films we approach the inevitable end of the picture. In total, the best side of "Bruce Lee, the Man, the Myth" is the reproduction of Lee's characteristic movements and the portrayal of fighting techniques which were closer to those of the star's martial arts background than the ones he was allowed to use in his own movies.

*

**Bruce's circling kick from "Enter..."
used the same principle as the Judo
stomach throw. He 'threw' himself
in order to 'throw' his opponent.**

"Bruce Lee Fights Back From The Grave" is a different kettle of fish. Not much can be said in its favour. It starts with an apparent strike of lightning on what appears to be Bruce Lee's grave stone. After that, the film goes downhill! Bruce K. L. Lea is supposed to be Bruce Lee resurrected(?), reincarnated(?) and working with a friend running a Kung Fu kwoon for a living. Unlike Bruce Li, Bruce K. L. Lea does not remotely resemble the star and neither the dubbing of his voice, nor of the voices of any of the actors and actresses helps very much. Several of the voices sound the same, possibly because the same actors dubbed the voices of several characters? Their tones of voice drone on through-out the picture, giving it a dirge-like quality which really drags.

The story(?) is not clear. The chief bad guys are a "white man, a black man, a Japanese, a Mexican," and... You've got it, they are all people who put the Chinese nation down, and Bruce K. L. Lea is going to teach them, as representatives of racism, a real lesson. In one scene defying belief, Lea catches a Japanese sword between what look like the soles of his feet. That would be something! The soles must have been made of rubber threaded with Toledo steel... In true Kung Fu movie style the bad guys endure kicks and punches from Lea which would have felled an elephant, then get up and carry on fighting.

The lighting in the film is something to see. In one scene for instance, Lea is fighting at night, then, when a technique is shown in slow motion, it is suddenly broad daylight, and then night again. I did once read of a wrestling contest which went on for nine hours, but surely not even this film would make a cut and expect the audience to realise it was show-ing a scene nine hours later.

Characteristically, drugs are the major cause of all the trouble in the plot, and characteristically the hero turns his back on the lure of wealth. He sticks to his Kung Fu principles whilst his former partner succumbs to temptation. Love interest is provided by a nice college girl, Caucasian though she be, as she likes Chinese people. She dies accidentally as Lea despatches his penultimate enemy, a cowboy with skin tight leather trousers. When Lea is in the depths of despair he actually drinks a lot of whiskey whilst some heavy belly dancing is going on, just to show how deep his despair really is. All in all, this epic is a waste of celluloid. As we have seen, there are more such films.

In the final analysis of course, films will be made only if people go to see them. Few directors and producers want to commit financial suicide. So if a film is not worth seeing, and fans want better films, the thing to do is not go to see them, and not buy or hire the videos. It is usually called boycotting. Like any other product, if people refuse to buy then the manufacturers will not make. At the time, the Bruce Lee fever gripped people, and their capacity to discrimi-nate was on hold until the fever abated.

CASS MAGDA

One "descendant" of Bruce Lee, pupil of Dan Inosanto who built on JKD and followed the master into the film world too.

DEBT TO INOSANTO

Cass Magda, a world class martial artist and teacher is well regarded in JKD circles having achieved a high degree of excellence under the personal tutelage of Dan Inosanto and later, other instructors. Cass trained with Dan Inosanto for 10 years and five of those years included being his personal assistant and constant companion on seminars worldwide and teaching at his two Academies in Los Angeles. Cass had this to say about his former mentor, "He taught me to use JKD as a method of study, to find the common threads in all styles, and most importantly just to love the martial arts with all your being, all your soul like he does. It was a priceless experience to be with him personally all those years."

MAGDA INSTITUTE

In 1983, Cass had become a champion full-contact stick fighter by winning four first place titles and two second place titles. In 1998 Cass celebrated the 10th anniversary of his school, the Magda Institute in Reseda, California, a suburb of Los Angeles. As an instructor, Cass has received much attention and notoriety world wide. He has been teaching in over 40 cities in the USA, Canada, Australia and Europe. He conducts teaching tours yearly in Europe and has a major martial arts following in England, Germany, Spain, France, Scandinavia, Italy and Greece. He has built up an impressive array of professional instructors who are teaching the Magda Institute program of JKD, Filipino Kali, and Indonesian Silat. His close disciple since 1985 Dave Carnell, runs a full time professional school in Stoke on Trent, UK.

JKD NUCLEUS

Cass has continued to train and research JKD by training with original students such as Ted Wong, Dan Lee and Bob Bremer. In 1998 Cass was asked to join the Board of Directors of the Jun Fan Jeet Kune Do

Cass Magda Institute for studying martial arts.

Cass Magda training with Guro Dan Inosanto (r).

Nucleus, an exclusive highly prestigious non-profit organization composed of all the original students of Bruce Lee from the three eras of his development - Seattle, Oakland and Los Angeles. Led by Linda Lee Cadwell (Bruce Lee's Widow) their goal is to preserve the teachings of Bruce Lee as it was taught to them and serve as an educational repository of knowledge of JKD. Cass says, "I hope to make a contribution to help preserve the essential teachings of Bruce Lee in their most authentic form as possible. I'm excited about the chance to get to know personally all these students of Bruce and learn from their experiences."

MORE SCOPE

Since the early eighties Cass has deepened and widened his martial art studies to include Gracie Jujitsu, Thai Boxing under Surachai Sirisute, Filipino Escrima under Raymundo Marquez, Lucky LucayLucay and Leo Giron, and numerous Indonesian Pentjak Silat styles under Paul deThouars and Herman Suwanda. His specialty has since become Indonesian Pentjak Silat. Cass says "Silat is a true self-defense combative system. It offers a practical system of philosophy and techniques that can be improvised upon as the situation dictates. The variety, richness and diversity of styles make this a fascinating and at the same time a truly unforgiving art."

He became the subject of a personal comic strip Kali Warrior, published in Martial Arts Illustrated magazine UK, using the Filipino arts as the action material. He launched a state of the art web site in June 1998 and in the first six months had nearly one million hits! He has appeared on the covers of 12 magazines worldwide and has authored or been featured in over 14 languages in over 45 countries. He has taught many celebrities including Rickki Rocket from Poison, Nikki Sixx from Motley Crue, Jake. E. Lee (Badlands), Blake Edwards (producer) and also served as a bodyguard to multi-platinum rocker Ozzy Osbourne for a brief period during one of his tours.

Cass now has an acting career and has spent considerable time working at famed Roger Corman studios as a stunt coordinator and choreographer. The martial arts roles in small films and commercials came easily to Cass and it wasn't long before he was starring in a film of his own with the release of Hawk's Vengeance in 1997 by Lions Gate/Dimension films (Miramax).

As a Guru (teacher) and artist Cass Magda continues to make a profound impact not only in the world of martial arts, but much like his own icon, Bruce Lee, in the lives of every student and observer he touches.

"Bad guy" Cass Magda doing his stuff against two attackers in "Hawk's Vengeance".

BRUCE LEE MET AND WAS A FRIEND TO CARTER HWANG

King of Kung Fu, Bruce Lee, is seen here in 1972 with Carter Hwang - photo courtesy of Richard Dean, European Monkey King.

A regular martial artist in the pages of K.O.A. was Richard Dean, based in Austria. Dean was well known as a teacher of Monkey Style Kung Fu and knew the film star and martial artist Carter Hwang. The latter was also fated to pass away at an early age.

Dean went to the opening of Carter's new training gym in Hong Kong in 1972 and was able to interview the star at length about his plans and prospects. Dean himself attained amazing agility and skill in Monkey style and was always welcomed by martial artists in Hong Kong. He conducted seminars in England, and wrote his famous book, 'Basic Monkey Boxing', which has been sold all over the world. He spoke of Carter Hwang as "a Kung fu brother".

Richard Dean, Bruce J. Lee (Li-Chan-Long) and Carter Hwang at the opening of the latter's new Hong Kong gym. (l. to r.). Photo courtesy of Richard Dean.

Carter Hwang used more traditional Kung Fu techniques in his films. He shared with Richard Dean a love of the traditional methods. Here he is in 'pre-fighting posture'. Photo courtesy Richard Dean.

ANIMAL STYLES

(photos: Chris Capstick)

Taking it literally! In May 1975 K.O.A. featured a man in Leeds, Ron Stone, who owned a young lion. He was observing it's fighting methods to see if he could develop a new Kung Fu style from the way it fought him!

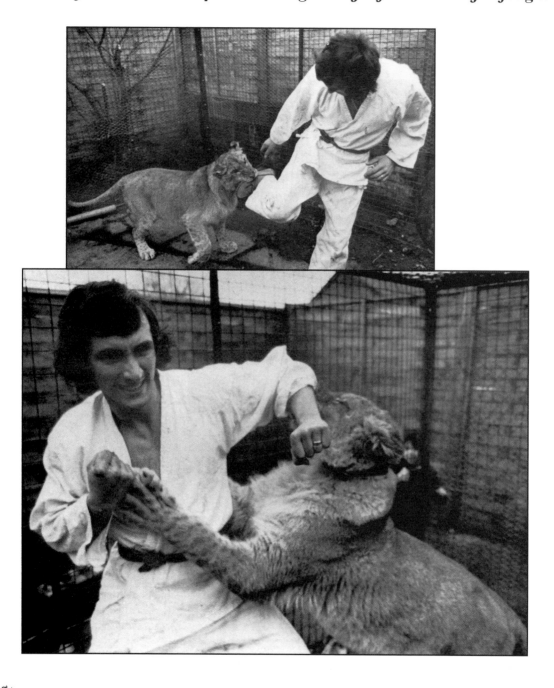

"The Big Boss"

Themes common to Chinese Kung Fu movies are echoed in this Bruce Lee 'show piece'.

There was a song in the wild west film, "Rancho Notorious", starring Marlene Dietrich, Jose Ferrer and Arthur Kennedy which has a line with the phrase, "hate, murder and revenge..."

It is fair to say that in many Chinese martial arts movies these are the themes. Sometimes the bad guys are Japanese. This is understandable because as everyone knows the Japanese invasion of China and the massacres which took place made an indelible imprint on the minds of the nation. No one was a better choice for a villain than a Japanese, as far as the Hong Kong fans were concerned. Other targets for revenge and humiliation were western strong men, western boxers, western sailors and foreigners in general. When one of these bites the dust in a Kung fu movie, the audience feels a strong sense of personal satisfaction.

In "Enter The Dragon" Lee defeats the westerner Oharra, but his main antagonist Han is Chinese, as are the majority of his "extra" opponents. In his earlier film "The Big Boss" all the enemies are mainly local Chinese bad guys. But the big enemy is of course drugs.

In watching this film again in December 1998, one cannot help seeing it in comparison with Kung Fu movies made after its first appearance, influenced by western technical skill and money. It has not worn well. The fight scenes in long shot are not good. The technical expertise of most of the fighters is low. Only the main characters display skill, and as said elsewhere this detracts from the standing of the skilful fighters because their opponents are, in boxing terms, literally no match for them. The dialogue is poor, the editing cursory, the lighting erratic, and so forth and so on. The penultimate scene where Lee dispatches the chief villain is sickeningly sadistic, and detracts from his character as a martial artist.

It may be part of the genre, but what always gets up my nose as a martial artist is how in the main the characters recover miraculously from their *injuries. Smashed, slashed, bashed, mashed, crashed, splashed, trashed and actually punched and kicked very, very hard, they spring to their feet as if nothing had happened. Their powers of recovery seem to depend on the story. If the story requires that the hero fights for ten minutes then the villains must survive for ten minutes. If the hero must deliver fifteen roundhouse kicks and ten back kicks, then the villains must endure such a number and get back up on to their feet, no matter how bad they feel, no matter how many cracked ribs, broken legs, concussed skulls, sprained ankles and other trifling injuries they have sustained. The show must go on. Full credit to the film makers on one score though. Bruce Lee does actually get hit, and injured. He is not shown as immune from the attacks of villains.*

In similar vein the plot is preposterous. One loses count, but over a dozen people are murdered, over a period of what appears to be several days, their bodies encased in ice or left lying around, and not a single report is made to the police or anyone in authority. In fact, apart from the police who do finally appear, there seems to be no one else around except the bad guys and the good guys. This may be why no one notices when prolonged knife fights are taking place in the front garden overlooking a main road; fights involving about a dozen men. One supposes that passers-by, if there were any, would simply glance at the mayhem and shrug their shoulders.

Is this type of criticism fair? I think so. Seriously, if the fans can still look at this film and admire it as a whole, then they really are fans. The standard of excellence in Hong Kong movies at the time varied. Comparatively, budgets were microscopic. But this does not explain the adulation and praise heaped on "The Big Boss" by fans who have seen far superior work. Love is blind, goes the saying, and this must include fan-love. Not having viewed "The Big Boss" for a long time, I had more or less forgotten its content in any detail. What Bruce Lee had said and written, and what his pupils and their pupils had said and written, formed the major part of my memories and impressions of the star. Seeing this film again made me realise once more that there is a tremendous gap between Lee's quest, his martial arts, his notes and essays, and the films he made.

Whether he would ever have been able to realise on film what he wrote and taught is a question for debate. He might possibly, with the help of admirers in the film industry, have brought strong elements of this on to the screen, but we shall never know. In any case, whatever he might have done, it would certainly have been superior to "The Big Boss". Difficulties in production were many, including the effects of old injuries plaguing Bruce Lee, and constant disputes with the director. Traditions of Chinese theatre, it is claimed, played their part in the way the film was made. For me, it is only as a piece of Bruce Lee archive material that it has any value.

Kung Fu Uniforms

Every new change in film costume made by Bruce Lee became an instant "must" for his thousands of student-followers.

Like every pop idol, the martial arts idol has an effect on what the real martial arts fan is wearing, in the training hall or kwoon. Tee shirt, Mandarin jacket, especially with white cuffs, and later the "Game of Death" leotard-like yellow outfit with the stripes down the sides became *de rigeur.*

As usual the K.O.A. shop and mail order department were inundated with calls for these sartorial items, but for the most part we left sales to the actual importers who were selling at exhorbitant prices. We were constantly amazed at what fans would do and pay to get into the right gear.

Funnily enough, the far eastern manu-facturers of uniforms were not familiar with western sizes, and there was peri-odic chaos in fitting people out with the right size. Kung fu shoes were another problem where sizing was concerned and it was some time before this was regulated. In one long summer the uni-form made by one company went com-pletely out of stock, as far as Europe was concerned, and an enterprising manu-facturer produced a similar uniform and stuck a fake label on it. We did not sell it. No one batted an eyelid as far as I could tell. When the original real suits returned to the market it was business as usual.

The "Game of Death" leotard or track suit was a one piece outfit. The ones on sale in England were made of a very stretchy material and looked like s--- . I could never imagine anyone ever wearing one. Bruce Lee's track suit of course was tai-lored to fit. The most popular clothing line was the Mandarin suit in black or navy blue or dark blue with the *white cuffs showing.* The few suits K.O.A. shop sold were always preceded by the request from the customer, "It's got to have the white cuffs showing, like Bruce Lee's." *White cuffs showing* became an in phrase; people who talked in their sleep could be heard mumbling it in the small hours of the morning. There must be many a mid-dle-aged former fan who will smile when he remembers this, and his own youthful enthusiasms. The jacket itself had the now familiar mandarin collar curving up in front of the chin, and the sleeves, in black, were too long. You had to turn them back a few inches to reveal *the white cuffs showing...*

Sometimes, the inside of the collar was white too. The jacket was fastened by a series of toggles, and it was the devil's own job to fasten and unfasten these quickly. I used to advise customers to undo the top two then pull the darned thing over their heads like a pullover! Some suits were made of cotton, some in polyester and some in a mixture. 'Toggles' were small loops with knots fitted to push through them. The knots wore down and the toggles became loose. What someone should have done, as was done with Taekwondo uniforms, was to make a pullover type jacket with toggles stitched in for effect. A lot of mothers, grandmothers, girl friends and wives would have been very grateful.

Tee-shirts were another craze, with JKD or a Yin-Yang symbol printed on, or just plain white. Plain white was popular among Wing Chun students and echoed Bruce Lee's attire in some of his pre-Enter the Dragon films.

What manufacturers noticed over a period of years was that the demand for uniforms of all description went up with regard to size. Whilst in the early days the most popular size was a 3, which fitted what we would now call a small man, requests went up to mainly size 4 and then even bigger. I put it down to all the vitamins and hamburgers that the younger generation were putting away during their adolescence.

Prices were another striking subject. It was obvious that they were always too high. Suits which sold overseas for one price fetched several times that price in Britain. There were several legitimate reasons for this including differences in exchange rates. But another reason was the old profit motive. As I had had no previous business experience prior to starting K.O.A. and opening the shop, I didn't have the faintest notion of what percentages were involved. It boggled my mind what some manufacturers regarded as a fair mark up. Let's leave the details to the Inland Revenue or I.R.S. depending on where you live.

Bruce Lee's gloves, as worn at the beginning of "Enter the Dragon", were another noteworthy phenomenon. Quickly, very quickly, they were on the market. We ordered some for the shop and I examined them. You had to squeeze your hand inside with a couple of shoe horns or failing that two tyre levers. As for making a fist, forget it. What did customers do with them when they had them, I don't know. Maybe they just looked at themselves in the mirror. If you had punched anything solid with them you would have broken your fingers.

Of course, whatever uniform you wore and however you cut your hair, you just could not look like Bruce Lee. The only thing left was to imitate his facial expressions and his haunting cries as he despatched his attackers. The latter explained the rumour that werewolves were roaming in Hyde Park in London, and on the Yorkshire moors. What other explanation could there be?

Bruce Lee Films in Context

The history of martial arts cinema was commemorated in Hong Kong in 1980 under the auspices of the Urban Council in the shape of the Fourth Hong Kong International Film Festival. Part of the event was a showing of no less than twenty-eight films of the genre dating from 1949 up to 1978. The programme notes were compiled by Lau Shing-Han, who said about "The Big Boss", that Bruce Lee's "stylisation of violence is shot through with an element of self mockery. Beneath the veneer of his heroism lie the dialects of *yin* and *yang*". Below are details of the films shown with a brief resume of each title.

INTRODUCTION

What the Chinese call *wu xia pian* constitute an important and distinctive genre within the Chinese cinema. The earliest example was the *Burning of the Red Lotus Monastery* series, produced in Shanghai from 1928. In the term *wu xia*, 'wu' denotes fighting or combat, and 'xia' connotes chivalry and valour. The commonly-used term *'kung-fu'* derives from Cantonese vernacular, and its use nowadays in connection with martial arts generally refers to unarmed combat.

We have been led to concentrate on unarmed combat films this year by the great number and variety of *wu xia pian* produced in Hong Kong; swordplay and armed combat films will be examined at a future time. We hope our specialisation will enable us to examine our subject in some depth. We must necessarily exclude the swordplay films of King Hu, Chang Cheh and Chu Yuan. However, in the course of our study, we try as far as possible to take account of the genre's overall development.

- Lau Shing-Hon

PROGRAMME NOTES

The True Story of Huang Fei-Hong: Whiplash Snuffs the Candle Flame

Dir: Hu Pang Scr: Wu Yixiao Martial Arts Instr: Liang Yongxiang
Cast: Guan Dexing, Ceo Dahua, Li Lan, Yuen Siu-Tin
Prod. Co: Yong Yao l6mm B/W 1949 (Cantonese dialogue; no subtitles)

The first in the series of over 80 Huang Fei-Hong films, this introduces Huang's family background and his martial artistry, the latter learned from the tradition of the Shaolin Monastery. It also establishes Huang's lasting 'image': as an ideal ethical model, embodying the Confucian virtues of Wisdom, *Jen* (benevolence) and Courage; as a strict *sifu* to his disciples. as a paragon of self-restraint. who uses violence only as the final resort; and as a moral pillar, who resists advances from women.

How Huang Fei-Hong Pitted a Lion Against the Unicorn

Dir: Hu Pang Scr: Hu Wensen Martial Arts Instr: Zeng Zhenhua
Cast: Guen Dexing, Ceo Dahua, Shi Jian, Ran Yen
Prod. Co: Qilin 35 mm B/W 1956 (Cantonese dialogue; no subtitles)

By 1956, the characters of Huang Fei-Hong and his disciples were very well established with the Cantonese cinema audience, and the year marked the climax of the series' popularity, This story begins in Kiangsi in the Bamboo Forest Temple, headquarters of an anti-Qing revolutionary organisation headed by Elder Red Brow, the originator of the Mantis School. Hounded by the Qing court, the Elder and his disciples take refuge in the Big Buddha Temple in Canton and there come into conflict with Huang when a local (played by the series' perennial villain Shi Jian) stirs up trouble between the two parties.

Huang Fei-Hong Wins the Dragon-boat Race

Dir: Hu Pang Scr: Wang Fang
Cast: Guan Dexing, Shi Jian, Ran Yen, Lin Jiao
Prod. Co: Jin Qiao 35 mm B/W 1956 (Cantonese dialogue; no subtitles)

Apart from possessing a structural unity found in few other films in the series, this film raises some interesting moral questions. The story deals with the rivalry between two villages in the annual Dragon-Boat Race, and with Huang's involvement in the conflict. Huang finally takes part in the Race himself, not to compete but to persuade the villains (a rich landlord and his son, played by Li Pengfei and Shi Jian respectively) to mend their ways, It is worth remarking that the young Liu Chia-Liang plays an important supporting character

Huang Fei-Hong's Greatest Fight

Dir: Hu Pang Scr: Wang Fang
Cast: Guan Dexing, Ceo Dahua, Ran Yen, Liu Zhan
Prod. Co: Lien He 35 mm BIW 1958 (Cantonese dialogue; no subtitles)

The great popularity of the Huang Fei-Hong series (in Singapore and Malaysia as well as Hong Kong) led producers to extract spectacular scenes from earlier films in the series and edit them into this opportunistic compendium of highlights. Sequences include; a cricket-fight (rarely seen nowadays), a cock-fight, Huang Fei-Hong leading a Lion Dance against four rival lions and managing to secure the lucky money from a stone crevice, and Huang engaging in combat with a huge, highly ornate dragon, manipulated by a large team of dancers, The most engaging scene, however, is a Centipede Dance (a tradition that is now probably lost), taken from *Huang Fei-Hong: The Iron Rooster versus the Centipede*. An extract from *Huang Fei-Hong Saves the Bride at Xiguan* shows Gust Dexing's expertise with the rod and also graphically demonstrates Huang's nobility of character: he takes no pride in his final victory and regrets having used violence, unavoidable though it was.

The Young Swordsman 'Lung Kim Fei' (Parts I and II)

Dir: Ling Yun Scr: Situ An Martial Arts Instr: Yuen Siu-Tin
Cast: Ceo Dahua, Yu Suqiu, Han Ying-Chieh
Prod. Co: Fulai 35 mm B/W with hand-tinted colour sequences 1964 (Cantonese dialogue; no subtitles)

This film is chosen to represent the 'fantastic' martial arts film of the mid-60s. Part I describes how the slow-witted Ceo Dahua is beaten and disfigured by a girl, his junior fellow-disciple. and is carried off by a roc to the Dark Lord of Fire, who instructs him in the eight forms of the Ru Lai Palm (each of which is represented by a different hand-coloured tint). The most powerful form is the Million Buddha Palm. Armed with this instruction, the youth returns to earth to seek his revenge. Part II features a variety of gadgets and fantastic fighting scenes, bringing together such elements as robots, Luo Han formations, mythical beasts, the Ru Lai Palm itself and the invincible flying rings in one cataclysmic battle. Though the form approximates science-fiction, the film's resolution hinges on highly traditional ethical concepts.

Huang Fei-Hong: The Invincible Lion-dancer
Dir: Wang Fang Scr: Situ An Martial Arts Instr: Guan Dexing, Shi Jian, Yuen Siu-Tin Cast: Guen Dexing, Shi Jian, Zeng Jiang, Yuen Woo Ping
Prod. Co: Yule 35 mm B/W 1968 (Cantonese dialogue; no subtitles)

Within an unusually coherent structural framework, this film offers an extensive exploration of Confucian ideas. It opens with a scene of Huang's birthday celebrations, where Huang's speech details the need for filial piety before heaven, earth, one's country, one's parents and one's teacher. Huang's principles are put to the test when he confronts the oppression of a helpless girl by the villain (Shi Jian); torn between his reluctance to resort to violence and his wish to help the girl, he faces an inner turmoil.

Huang Fei-Hong: The Eight Bandits
Dir: Wang Feng Scr: Situ An Martial Arts Instr: Guan Dexing, Shi Jian,
Yuen Siu-Tin
Cast: Guen Dexing, Shi Jian, Zeng Jiang, Zhang Yiogcei
Prod. Co: Yule 35 mm B/W 1968 (Cantonese dialogue; no subtitles)

Repeated conflicts between Huang Pal-Hong's disciples and villain Shi Jian's Eight Bandits force Huang to make a firm stand for his principles. The film explores both Huang's inner tensions and the villain's character in some depth. Of special interest is the clash of Huang's Drunken Fist with villain Yuen Siu-Tin's Monkey Fist. The ending evokes memories of *King Hu's Reining in the Mountain*.

Huang Fei-Hong: The Duel against the Black Rascal
Dir: Wang Fang Scr: Situ An Martial Arts Instr: Guen Dexing, Shi Jian,
Yuen Siu-Tin
Cast: Guen Dexing, Shi Jian, Li Hong, Zhou Ji
Prod. Co: Yule 35 mm B/W 1968 (Cantonese dialogue; no subtitles)

In terms of plot. perhaps one of the best in the Huang Pal-Hong series. Shi Jian this time plays a conceited man, not malicious at heart, who firmly believes in the power of the fist; his principle is "the world is what you make of it". Huang recognises his worth and recommends him as instructor to a martial arts school, but the Shi Jian character is soon corrupted by his new position and starts annexing territories to create an underworld empire. Huang finally contrives to reform him, and the manner of his reformation includes an interesting twist.

Huang Fei-Hong's Combat with the Five Wolves
Dir: Wang Fang &r: Situ An Martial Arts Instr: Guan Dexing, Shi Jian,
Yuen Siu-Tin
Cast: Guan Dexing, Shi Jian, Mel Guinu, Zeng Jiang
Prod. Co: Yule 35 mm B/W/Scope 1969 (Cantonese dialogue; no subtitles)

The film language. the narrative structure and the sketching of character and atmosphere are all quite mature. The fight scenes are more authentically Chinese in style than those in many contemporary Mandarin *wu xia plan*. Huang's duel with a samurai) anticipates equivalent scenes in the films of Wang Yu and Bruce Lee. The set for Shi Jian's headquarters has similarities with the pirate base in King Hu's *The Valiant Ones*. Although approaching the 70s, the character of Huang Pal-Hong is still shown to treat his enemies with martial virtue, sincerity and forgiveness.

From the Highway
Dir: Chang Tseng-Chei Scr: Sima Zhong- Yuen Martial Arts Instr: Ho Hsiung
Cast: Yang Chun, Ingrid Hu, Sun Yueh
Prod. Co: Cathay 35 mm Colour/Scope 1970 (Mandarin dialogue; English subtitles)

Set in Northern China in early Republican days, this film has a brusqueness quite distinct from *kung-fu* films about the South. The story centres on a bandit raid on the Camp of An, carried out with the complicity of an infiltrator inside the camp (played by Sun Yueh, making lethal use of his pigtail). and the subsequent rout of the bandits by the Rider of the White Steed (Yang Chun). The film has rich production values and a fine grasp of atmosphere. especially in scene of the raid on the camp. Other attractive features include a spectacular array of popular art forms of the period (street-balled singing, nickelodeons, puppet shows, Honan Drumming and monkey shows).

Vengeance
Dir: Chang Cheh Scr: I Kuang, Chang Cheh Martial Arts Instr: Teng Chia, Yuan Hsiang-Jen Cast: David Chiang, Ti Lung, Wang Ping
Prod. Co: Shaw Brothers 35 mm Colour/Scope 1970 (Mandarin dialogue; English subtitles)

Chang Cheh's best production in terms of its use of film language, **Vengeance** also breaks with the tradition of showing opera performers of early Republican China passively accepting oppression from the warlords. Here, David Chiang seeks bloody revenge for the death of his elder brother (Ti Lung). A hauntingly tragic mood prevails in the scene of Ti Lung's ambush.

The Chinese Boxer
Dir/Scr: Wang Yu Martial Arts Instr: Tang Chia
Cast: Wang Yu, Lo Lieh, Chen Hsing
Prod. Co: Shaw Brothers 35 mm Colour)Scope 1970 (Mandarin dialogue;
English subtitles)

Although unmistakably influenced by Japanese samurai movies in its emphasis on blood and violence, the film is at the same time intended as a direct challenge to the popular Japanese film *Judo Saga*. Set in early Republican China, it traces the course of Wang Yu's tortuous training in Iron Palm and Weightlessness techniques, through to his ultimate victory over the murderers of his sifu, Japanese judo and karate experts.

The Big Boss
Dir/Scr: Lo Wel Martial Arts Instr: Han Ying-Chieh
Cast: Bruce Lee, Nora Miao, Han Ying-Chieh, James Tien
Prod. Co: Golden Harvest 35 mm Colour/Scope 1971 (Mandarin dialogue;
English subtitles)

Bruce Lee's grace and inner resources make this considerably more than a formulary martial arts movie. He embellishes his fight scenes with such touches as savouring his own blood, or beating up the body of the man he has just killed and then falling on top of it. His stylisation of violence is shot through with an element of self-mockery. Beneath the veneer of his heroism lie the dialectics of *yin* and *yang*.

The Casino
Dir: Chang Tseng-Chai Scr: I Kuang Martial Arts Instr: Liang Shao-Lung
Cast: Ho Li-Li, Yueh Hue, Shi Jian (Shih Kien)
Prod. Co: Shaw Brothers 35 mm Colour/Scope 1972 (Mandarin dialogue;
Engllsh subtitles

When the Yueh Hue character steps into the casino, he not only out-bluffs villain Shih Klan, but also manages to win the entire casino and its owner, Ho Li-Li. But as Lao Tea says. "There is tragedy embedded in every happiness". The young man's good fortune proves to be the beginning of a series of bloody misfortunes.

King Boxer
Dir: Chang Chang-Ho &r: Chiang Yang Martial Arts Instr: Lau Kar-Wing
Cast: Lo Lieh, Wang Ping, Tung Lin
Prod. Co: Shaw Brothers 35 mm Colour/Scope 1972
(Mandarin dialogue;
English subtitles)

With a Chinese cast and a Korean director, this film spearheaded the advance of *kung-fu* films into the international market. (It was distributed in the USA as *Five Fingers of Death*, in France as *La Main de fer* and in the UK as *King Boxer*.) It resembles *The Chinese Boxer* in structure, although it climaxes with a martial arts tournament rather than a duel. One curious feature is that Lo Lieh (a veteran player of villains) end Tung Lin (the serene monk in King Hu's *Raining in the Mountain*) here exchange their usual roles.

The Bloody Fists
Dir: Ng See Yuen Scr: I Kuang Martial Arts Instr: Yuen Woo-Ping,
Yuan Hsiang-Jen
Cast: Chen Hsing, Chen Kuan-Tai, Henry Yue Young
Prod. Co: Empire Cinema Centre 35 mm Colour/Scope 1972 (Mandarin
dialogue; English subtitles)

This anti-Japanese kung-fu film was Hg See-Yuen's directorial debut, and its success as a low-budget independent production (shot entirely on location and using newcomers and martial artists in the leading roles) encouraged many other independent film-makers to follow suit. The film is characterised by brutal fight scenes, vivid character sketches and atmospherics.

Men of Iron
Dirs: Chang Cheh, Pao Hsueh-Li Scr: I Kuang, Chang Cosh
Martial Arts Instr: Liu Chia-Liang, Chen Chuan
Cast: Chen Kuan-Tai, Ching Li, Chu Mu
Prod. Co: Shaw Brothers 35 mm Colour/Scope 1972
(Mandarin dialogue;
English subtitles)

A sequel to *The Boxer from Shantung*, this is yet another tragic and violent portrait of a young man's rise in the underworld, set in early Republican Shanghai. The Chen Kuan-Tai character clashes with a gang boss (Yang Chi-Ching) over territory. and with the boss's son (Tien Ching) over a woman (Ching Li).

The Fate of Lee Khan
Dir: King Hu Scr: Wang Chung, King Hu Martial Arts Instr: Samo Hung
Cast: Li Li-Hue, Hsu Fang, Angela Mao, Roy Chiao
Prod. Co: King Hu Film Productions/Golden Harvest 35 mm Colour/Scope 1973 (Mandarin dialogue; English subtitles)

Reminiscent of (but more complex than) the Peking opera *The Midnight Confrontation (San Cha Kou)*, this King Hu film largely takes place in the Spring Inn, headquarters of an anti-Yuan resistance group, where the Ming heroes gather in a life-or-death struggle against Mongol Baron Lee Khan for a battle plan. A number of elements combine to make the film one of Hu's masterpieces; especially the scene in which Lea Khan and his sister listen to Han Ying-Chieh's rendition of *Valediction*, a scene of surface elegance that pulses with hidden intimations of death.

The Valiant Ones
Dir/Scr: King Hu Martial Arts Instr: Samo Hung
Cast: Hsu Fang, Pal Ying, Roy Chiao, Hang Ying-Chieh
Prod. Co: King Hu Film Productions 35 mm Colour/Scope 1975
(Mandarin dialogue: English subtitles)

As Tony Rayns has pointed out, this story of resistance against Sino-Japanese pirates in the Ming Dynasty has surprising affinities with the plot of the PRC film *The Opium War*. Through the use of stylised repetitions of actions in the fight scenes between Roy Chiao and Han Ying-Chieh, and between Pal Ying and Samo Hung, King Hu introduces an abstract, aesthetic dimension to the genre. A chef d'oeuvre in the use of film language!

The Spiritual Boxer
Dir: Liu Chia-Liang &r: I Kuang Martial Arts Instr: Liu Chia-Liang
Cast: Wong Yu, Lin Chen-Chi, Ti Lung, Chen Kuan-Tai
Prod. Co: Shaw Bros. 35 mm Colour/Scope 1975
(Mandarin dialogue;
English subtitles)

The true progenitor of the other *kung-fu* comedies of the 70s; the extent of its influence can be measured by the frequency with which such scenes as Wong Yu's solicitation of spirits to perform the Monkey Fist and the feminine Lin Daiyu Fist or the drunken *sifu* instructing his disciple in Shaolin techniques have been imitated. The film's fluency bears witness to director Liu Chia-Liang's expertise in the field of Chinese martial arts and to his awareness of the dynamics of popular comedy.

The Himalayan
Dir: Huang Fang Scr: I Kuang Martial Arts Instr: Samo Hung, Hen Ying-Chieh
Cast: Chen Hsing, Angeia Mao, Dorian Tan, Samo Hung
Prod Co: Golden Harvest 35 mm Colour/Scope 1976
(Mandarin dialogue;
English subtitles)

Shot in Nepal, the film describes Chen Hsing's unscrupulous seizure of power and the revenge of Angela Mao and Dorian Tan after painstaking training in the Mi School of martial arts. The plot structure is exceptionally well organised, especially where Chen's Machiaveillian strategies are concerned.

The Secret Rivals
Dir: Ng See- Yuan Scr: Dong Lu, Ng See-Yuan Martial Arts In:str: Li Mingwen,
Zhang Quan
Cast: Liu Chung-Liang, Wang Tao, Huang Chang-Li
Prod. Co: Seasonal Film Corporation 35 mm Colour/Scope 1976
(Mandarin dialogue; English subtitle:)

Based on a love/hate relationship between Southern Fist (Wang Tao) and Northern Kick (Liu Chung-Liang), the film's thematic structure approximates that of a set of Chinese boxes as it explores its intricacies of love, friendship and hate. Both lead actors demonstrate expert artistry in their martial techniques, lending the climax (in which they unite in a joint attack on Iron Fox, played by Huang Chang-L) a fierce excitement.

The Good, The Bad and The Loser
Dir/Scr: Mak Kar Martial Arts Instr: Lau Kar-Wing
Cast: Lau Kar-Wing, Roy Chiao, Huang Jiawei
Prod. Co: Advance Film Ltd 35 mm Colour/Scope 1976
(Cantonese dialogue;
English subtitles)

This film was instrumental in establishing parody as a new sub-genre within *kung-fu* cinema, replete with a large measure of caricature. At its core is an 'odd couple' relationship between a doltish monk (Roy Chiao) and a small-time fraud (Lau Kar-Wing), the latter forever taking advantage of the former.

Snake in the Eagle's Shadow
Dir: Yuen Woo-Ping Scr: Ng See- Yuan, Shao Lung, Teal Chi-Kong Martial Arts Instr: Yuan Woo-Ping, Tsui Her
Cast: Jacky Chan, Yuen Siu-Tin, Shek Tin
Prod. Co: Seasonal Flim Corporation 35 mm Colour/Scope 1978
(Cantonese dialogue; English subtitles)

The huge box-office success of this first feature from martial arts instructor turned director Yuen Woo-Ping launched a wave of imitative *kung-fu* comedies. Its theme (a young, oppressed hero undergoes vigorous training under an eccentric master end subsequently avenges himself) is echoed in many other movies in the genre.

Dirty Tiger, Crazy Frog
Dir: Mak Kar Scr: Mak Kar, Chang Chi-Wai Martial Arts Instr: Lau Kar-wing, Samo Hung
Cast: Lau Kar-Wing, Samo Hung, Shek Tin
Prod. Co: Gar-Bo 35 mm Colour/Scope (Cantonese dialogue; English subtitles)

In spirit, a sequel to *The Good, the Bad and the Loser*. The Chinese title indicates the 'odd couple' relationship between Little Tiger (Lau Kar-Wing) and Frog Hung (Samo Hung). Characters and action are both caricatured to an even greater extent than in the earlier film, although the plot once again turns on the rivalry between the protagonists.

Drunken Master

(aka Drunk Monkey in the Tiger's Eye)
Dir: Yuen Woo Ping Scr: Ng See- Yuen, Hai Wa-An
Martial Arts Instr: Yuan Woo-Ping, Tsui Har
Cast Jacky Chan Yuen Siu-Tin, Huang Chang-LI
Prod Co: seasonal film Corporation 35 mm Colour/Scope
197B
(Cantonese dialogue English subtitles)
　　Surpassing the structure of its predecessor **Snake in the Eagle's Shadow** this film remains the most commercially successful **kung-fu** comedy to date. The mischievousness of the young Huang Fei-Hong (played by Jacky Chan) leaves his father with no choice but to hand the boy over to Begger Su (Yuen Siu-Tin) to learn martial arts and self-discipline. Under Su's guidance, the boy finally defeats his formidable foe (Huang Chang Li) Sequences of special interest include the scene where sifu and disciple practice Drunken Fist while chanting Li Bai's poem **About to Drink Wine** in unison.

Dirty Kung-fu
Dir: Lau Kar-Wing Scr: I Kuang Martial Arts Instr: the Lau Brothers Cast: Wong Yu, Shek Tin, Choi Siu-Keung
Prod. Co: Lau Brothers 35 mm Colour/Scope 1978
(Cantonese dialogue; English subtitles)
　　Another film in the vein of **Dirty Tiger, Crazy Frog.** The characters live by bounty-hunting; their sole concern is with seeking advantages for themselves, to the total disregard of all moral questions. As the Shek Tin character says: "The point of life is to make money, and there are precious few chances". The central character (Wong Yu) is more a trickster than an authentic martial artist and, needless to say, the concept of honouring his **sifu** is quite beyond him; after picking up some martial techniques from eels, he cheerfully dines on them

Warriors Two
Dir: Samo Hung Scr: Situ An Martial Arts Instr: Samo Hung
Cast: Samo Hung, Liang Jiaren, Qia Longfa
Prod. Co: Golden Harvest 35 mm Colour/Scope 1978
(Cantonese dialogue;
English subtitles)
　　Although it retains all the formulary elements in its plotline (suffering oppression, learning martial arts under a **sifu,** vigorous training for revenge), this is Samo Hung's most integrated and coherent film. Both Liang Jiaren end Feng Kean are highly successful in their portrayals of hero and villain respectively. As Hg Ho has pointed out, the balance between the tragic end the comic in the Bamboo Forest revenge scene is a phenomenon rarely found in other **kung-fu** films.

Booking folder notes by Leu Shing-Hon. Translated by Marie Ho and Tony Rayns.

What became known in the film business as 'chop-sockies' had an enormous number of films behind them. With 'King Boxer' in 1971 the western world began to take notice of the immense success of Kung fu movies. Companies like Warner Bros. in the United States and Hammer Films in the United Kingdom leaped forward in the wake of tremendous film fan reaction. Virtually no westerners had ever seen the long incident filled fight scenes which were the back bone of such productions. They were thrilled and fascinated. What thrilled and fascinated western film companies were the profits. These came from the relatively small outlay needed to make the movies. For instance, 'Big Boss' cost $100,000 and quickly took $500,000 in Hong Kong alone. 'Fist of Fury' cost $200,000 and grossed about one million dollars. And after a brief two weeks of showing, 'The New

One-Armed Swordsman' took five times its initial cost of $50,000; tea money for a Hollywood epic. In London when the earlier Bruce Lee films were to be released I recall a short, dark haired youngish man representing Cathay Films handing out match books with publicity details printed on them. He was very excited about their new 'property' but seemed at a bit of a loss to say much; he just knew it was hot. He handed out film stills to the Press, including K.O.A. and held his his breath. How would English audiences react? He need not have worried...In the 1970's there were no less than ninety-seven cinemas in Hong Kong. Most of the population was under the age of twenty-five and poverty and illiteracy were rife. Film makers played on the needs of such people to get away from the sweat shop lives they led. Kung Fu movies gave them a simple villain to hate, a hero to love, and in their imagination a violent revenge by proxy on the causes of their own condition. This was one version of the underlying reasons for the genre's popularity. But, this simple equation did not correspond to the conditions of people living in countries where these exported films found their new marks. In the 1970's many western countries were relatively prosperous and revelling in a new sexual revolution. The fans were not working in sweat shops, they were not illiterate, though not college professors either. The Kung Fu movie had to have another explanation for its success.

There may be a complex of reasons. But one strand could be the long, continuous action of certain scenes. In most Hollywood films up to say 1970 a fight would not last very long. Very often it was a matter of a few punches and the villain would be down and out of the reckoning. Sword fights could last longer and move from one room to another or out into the open. It was mainly in Wild West movies that the longest fights took place using only bare hands, for instance between Alan Ladd and Van Heflin in "Shane". But the gun eventually decided everything.

Another strand was probably the way in which the violence was portrayed. Controversial films in this respect such as "The Wild Bunch" and "Straw Dogs" were very thin on the ground at the time, and violence was relatively muted. Exploding packets of blood and explicitly focussed sadistic scenes had yet to be given the green light of future decades. Audiences were probably as fascinated by the mere sight of prolonged violence in the Kung Fu genre as they were by the martial arts which were the vehicle for it. The final fight scene of "Big Boss" was a case in point. Bruce Lee the super fit star is one item in this scene, but another, just as powerful, is the feeling of pure hate, lasting for some minutes, coupled with that of satisfaction in inflicting pain and death on the big boss. The guardians of public taste, the censors, were coming to terms not with violence itself but the emotions which accompanied it.

Chinese martial arts films had no such hang ups. The living population, many of them, had first hand knowledge of violent and sadistic treatment at the hands of Japanese invaders and even members of their own society. It would be presumptuous to say that they were inured to it, who could be, but certainly their life experience was not comparable with that of many western film fans. If culture is "the sum total of things people do as a result of having been so taught" then the meeting of east - west in the martial arts film auditorium was a new learning experience for fans in Europe and the United States. Having "been so taught" they asked for more.

Former stunt man turned actor David Chiang expressed his disappointment with the Hong Kong film industry's preoccupation with the fantasy which was the basis of all their martial arts productions. He himself was tired of it, and said that he wanted to make films which would show the audiences the plight of the population. Poverty, inequality, exploitation and so on. Western audiences had been fed such films for many a long year; the change in the political and social climate following the end of the Second World War had seen to that. If Pinewood and Hollywood had any tradition it was one of diversity, compared with Hong Kong; a diversity which encompassed what David Chiang was looking for. Culture shock aptly describes the impact of Bruce Lee and the accompanying deluge of "chop-sockies".

They released pent up emotions in the fans, and even stirred the minds of many intellectuals surveying the scene, notwithstanding the regular derision which the latter produced like a knee jerk reaction to the very words "Bruce Lee". Behind it was the realisation that the Kung Fu film phenomenon's effects were a social indicator. One writer described the western response to the films as a break "with the arid bitterness of the American television-influence thriller (which) returned us to the swashbuckling fantasies of the costume film of twenty or thirty years before". For middle aged people this "return" might have had some literal substance, but for most fans it was not a return in that literal sense at all. They were too young. For them it was new, it was a break, it was another type of experience. Furthermore, the "swashbuckling fantasies" had never contained the explicit violence of the "chop-sockies". In the former films, death and injury took place almost invisibly. A sword thrust was delivered and a man died. A bullet struck home and a woman died. It happened like closing the lid of a box, and you did not see what was inside. In the newly arrived Kung Fu film you saw everything, up to a point. And that point was way down the line compared with the "swash-buckling fantasies".

What you did get in the earlier western films was emotion, that is, emotion with which a western audience could culturally identify. Someone dies, and there is emotion, even in action filled films. In Kung Fu movies the emotion is sometimes there but often scant and certainly less emphasised. It is like the British stiff upper lip gone mad. Obviously such thoughts could lead to an in depth analysis of differences between Chinese and European people and the processes of their emotional lives, going beyond the needs of this publication. But even so in my own contacts with Chinese people both from Hong Kong and the Mainland, the differences are great. Those whom I have met are very "single minded" compared with westerners. Like the heroes of the martial arts films they relentlessly pursue their goals and what they feel is kept in the background, taking second place. In the West, what we feel comes very much to the foreground, and it is only perhaps the economic pressures and their accompanying factors which are bringing this more ruthless or less sentimental attitude into our lives.

Bruce Lee's films and the majority of Kung Fu films always bring action as a solution to problems. In their case it is violent action. Though lip service is paid to the archetypal sage or master, he is in a sense part of the "classical mess". Perhaps we are still too close to the martial arts film phenomenon to be really able to put it into context. Even so it deserves more serious consideration.

At this same Hong Kong Film Festival were half a dozen films by new, young Chinese directors, including one martial arts film, 'The Butterfly Murders" directed by Tsui Hark. In an interview, the director said that they had tried to get "away from the orthodox Chinese Martial Arts world... Martial Arts films as they have existed so far are very limited in form, I feel." In his film he included elements of foreign film methods, with "futuristic" tones, and this was remarked upon by audiences and critics. This did not of course signal the end of the martial arts films "as they have existed" but it did indicate a New Wave of writing and directing, photography and editing, in which Bruce Lee might have eventually played a part.

(Note: film receipts quoted in this article are relative and we are not aware of the up to date figures - Ed.)

karate

AND ORIENTAL ARTS   75p

100TH ISSUE

In 1983 we reached our 100th issue of K.O.A. and celebrated by going into colour. Western knowledge of Eastern martial arts had really grown by leaps and bounds and our cover story was about the martial arts of Vietnam, called "Vo". It's origin is said to be Tibetan, and goes back several thousand years. The piece was supplied by Arepi.

VISIT TO LEE'S GRAVE

SHAOLIN ART OF COMBAT

WADO/SHOTOKAN ROUNDUP

ADVANCED WING CHUN

JULY • AUG 1981

karate

AND ORIENTAL ARTS   no 91   60p

One martial artist, Graham P. Williams, who was plainly also a graphic artist, sent in this meticulously drawn head of Bruce Lee which we used on the cover of K.O.A.

Death of Bruce Lee
and the Aftermath

People were genuinely shocked by the anouncement of Bruce Lee's death. Fans phoned K.O.A. offices for confirmation of the news but we knew as much as the callers. Very quickly the rumours began to circulate as to the cause of his death. These included the following theories:

1. Bruce Lee had died from a heart attack.
2. He had died from a combination of drug abuse and over exertion whilst training.
3. He had been poisoned by big time film producers because he would not sign up to work in their films.
4. He had been killed by 'dim mak' or the delayed death touch, a supposed martial arts technique in which a blow is struck and the victim succumbs at a specified time after the blow. This had been done as punishment for revealing Chinese martial arts secrets to westerners.
5. He had crossed Chinese gangsters.
6. He had been killed by a rival martial artist.
7. He had died from cannabis use.
8. He had died from brain swelling caused by a combination of aspirin and another drug.
9. It was all a publicity stunt and he was still alive.

The media thrives on rumours of course, and the media played up these stories for all they were worth, without any consideration for the Lee family and friends or the realities of the event. A famous pathologist was flown out to Hong

Kong and he put paid to all the theories, except theory no. 8 which he admitted was a distinct possibility. This expert opinion was much too prosaic for the majority of fans. They either wanted to believe that the star still lived or that he had died as a result of one of the other more novel explanations; one which could have very well been an episode from one of his films.

K.O.A. staff, including myself, were flabbergasted. The only comparable fan reaction we had come across was when *Inside Kung Fu* magazine had featured a picture of Elvis Presley consecutively on its covers, together with a story about The King's involvement in martial arts. These issues had gone like wildfire and the enthusiasm of the Elvis Presley Fan Club in England had been unbelievable. They bought as many as they could get. Maybe we at K.O.A. were a bunch of media snobs, but we just could not bring ourselves to join in the hooha about Lee's death, in print. The man was dead, the family and friends and pupils mourned him, period. Ten years later, on the anniversary of his death, we did print a few pages marking the event, but that was all.

Of course when a famous person dies, he or she is not there to affirm or deny anything written or said about him or her. So it was with Bruce Lee. Speculation, claims, assertions, criticisms and many other reactions followed. I think that those who had been close to Lee were bowled over by it all. Films using Bruce Lee's name followed in rapid succession, and films using part of the names of his films likewise. With Bruce Lee gone, followers turned to those nearest to him in martial arts: Dan Inosanto, James DeMile, Richard Bustillo, Jesse Glover, Cass Magda, and others had all shared in the star's life and art to some extent and they were quoted and misquoted out of hand. Publishers frantically searched for anyone and any written source so that they could jump on to the bandwagon and publish something about Lee. The whole martial arts world was lifted into a new, undreamed of popularity and K.O.A. staff watched it, bemused...

Much later, in 1979, "Inside Kung Fu" in its November issue presented an interview with James DeMile, written by Paul Maslak on the question of whether Bruce Lee was ever defeated. The former pupil stressed the insecurity of the star because of his small build, and said that it had to be impossible that Lee was ever beaten because "it would literally, psychologically have destroyed him". DeMile, a qualified psychologist and hypnotherapist gave a fair and human assessment of his teacher. It was balanced, it seemed to me, with none of the hero worship we had grown to expect in most accounts of the star's life. "So I *don't* believe it," DeMile stressed.

This very interesting and in a sense gripping interview went right to the centre of the Jeet Kune Do philosophy by claiming that when Bruce Lee found that he could not defeat his Kung Fu seniors using the same techniques as they used, he had to find alternatives. One of the examples of this was to change his Chi Sao of Wing Chun into Trapping Hands, or Phon Sao. DeMile made the point that when Bruce came to the U.S.A. and met really powerfully built people, "the bigger Americans had an aggressiveness and intensity which went right through Chi Sao."

When I first read this interview it pleased me enormously because it brought sanity and perspective into the whole Bruce Lee phenomenon. It did nothing to bring Bruce Lee or JKD down, in fact DeMile himself built on JKD, but it brought a coolness into the feverish atmosphere which had been sadly lacking. Wild criticism of Bruce Lee we had had in plenty; adulation in plenty. This was different.

The article went on to say that when Trapping Hands proved to have some limitations also, Lee produced a "spring load" method which gave an "endless isometric tension against... arms...and legs." This was more like it. It portrayed a martial artist, Lee, experimenting and inventing in pursuit of a faultless adaptable fighting art. This was the stuff of real life, not myth. Though only one page long, the piece was the most balanced I had ever read.

Later still in the October 1986 "Inside Kung Fu" an interview with John Saxon another intelligent and balanced offering appeared, in the Editorial. Here, Saxon spoke candidly and fairly about his experiences with the star. He described how Bruce had told him on the telephone that he had not been feeling at all well, and that "he had been fainting". At the end of the conversation Bruce said, "something very ominous". This was, "Maybe there won't be a Bruce Lee anymore".

Saxon too had been struck by the fact that Lee had become a myth. He recalled that on a television programme he had been asked to comment on Bruce Lee and had said that the latter had done the most to remove the "myths of the martial arts". Towards the end of the interview, Saxon remarked:

"But wouldn't it be ironic if we made a myth out of him."

MAR • APR 1981
karate
AND ORIENTAL ARTS no 89 60p

WHAT WILL BODIE DO NEXT? *See inside!*

English media stars such as Lewis Collins from the series "The Professionals" entered the martial arts arena. Here Collins poses for Jujutsu action with members of the British Jujutsu organisation. K.O.A. no. 89, March 1981 - photo provided by Sensei Richard Morris.

Andrew Stoker, twelve-year-old student of Ku...
year and visited the last r...

It was a hot day as we drove to the master...
The blossom on the trees was in full bloom, a...
us from the blazing sun. Suddenly, there it...
stance. (...

BI
NOVEMBER 27
FOUNDER

I felt a surge of sadness that he was no lo...
for a long time, as the birds sang and the leav...
and beyond it, and the hundre...

Though th
His s

The gravestone was red, with engraved wr...
headstone...

YOUR
CON
GUIDE
OUR
LIE

This touching scene shows a young English fan visiting the grave of Bruce Lee, with obvious respect, and regret at his passing. *(Published in 1981 issue no. 91)*

YC
DEV
I
ODY

don, England, went to Seattle in May of this
f his idol Bruce Lee ......

ke View Cemetery, Seattle, Washington.
ut of the car, and walked, the trees sheltered
olidly, like Bruce Lee himself in a fighting
e words:

E
JULY 20, 1973
KUNE DO

on the earth. I sat and gazed at the grave
d in the wind. There was a small bush nearby
raves, were white mountains.

has gone
ains

A white marble book lay at the foot of the
nscribed:

ATION
TO
VARD
NAL
ON

NG

EE'S

EY

PART TW0

FIGHTING INFLUENCES

Bruce Lee *and the* Great Wing Chun Explosion

In the late 1960's K.O.A. magazine had been running for a few years, and knowledge of Chinese Kung fu was still small in the West. Karate was spreading, with France leading the way, under the direction of Henri Plee, one of the trail blazers of martial arts in Europe.

I was contacted by a man called Rolf Clausnitzer, who was familiar with Hong Kong, and the martial arts and movie scene on the island. He began to talk to me about something called Wing Chun. He said it was a short range, powerful, attacking system, made famous by Grandmaster Yip Man. Rolf went on and on about Wing Chun. As an editor I was always looking out for something new to put in K.O.A. magazine, and as we were now publishing books, mainly to pay for running the mag., I listened to what he had to say.

He showed me some techniques, and I was impressed, mainly by one movement in which say a boxer's left jab or lead punch is pushed down by the Wing Chun expert's left front palm, to be followed by a rapid, straight punch straight down the middle, with the waiting right hand. Later I realised that this was the type of striking analysis of possibilities which Bruce Lee engaged in, for hours or days at a time. In the West it was new.

Rolf Clausnitzer explained one of the principle ideas of Wing Chun: to punch down the middle, centre line, of an opponent's body. Such punches were straight line attacks, the shortest distance between two points! Geometry used in a simple fashion. He showed me that Wing Chun blocking movements remain within the area outlined by an opponent's body.

A well known teacher of Wing Chun was Joseph Cheng. He was a colourful character who was bodyguard to Princes of the Middle East. Here he is posing as 007 with a lady at his feet.

Joseph Cheng, Austin Goh, Nigel Fan and Eddie Yeoh promoted Wing Chun also in Ireland, principally in the city of Dublin at the invitation of Wally Dylan of the North Wind Martial Arts Academy.

Cheng made a reputation for himself too in Liverpool, home of the Beatles and of the most famous Shotokan Karate fighting team of the Karate Union of Great Britain or K.U.G.B.

To simply survive in Liverpool you had to be a bit more determined than most people. Shop keepers had guard dogs to stop thieves breaking in through the roof to steal martial arts equipment! The bastards killed the dogs...

This principle later appeared in Lee's published writings. The more Rolf spoke the more interested I became. He told me that he had a Sifu, or teacher. This was Greco Wong, to whom Rolf later introduced me. Rolf wished very much to make Wing Chun known to the British martial arts community. But, alas, he was ahead of his time. Britons were still coming to terms with Shotokan Karate, Wado-ryu Karate, then Goju-ryu, and the style principally taught by Mas. Oyama and his students, Kyokushinkai, and later still with Shukokai, and Shotokai. We were not ready for Wing Chun.

In spite of this, I went along with Rolf and he continued to encourage my interest. I had done some Karate in the middle 1960's and I was used to slamming my forearms into powering blocks. The smooth, and in the early stages, difficult blocks of Wing Chun, using the wrists and elbows, seemed awkward to me. At that time I could not see how a small move can deflect a strong blow; like most westerners, I was just on the fringe at that time.

Still more barriers stood in the way of Wing Chun becoming known, as I was to discover. One day Rolf invited me to meet Greco Wong, a former pupil of Grandmaster Yip Man. We went to a Chinese restaurant near London's Chinatown and were served with bean curd soup. I had never tasted it before. It was quite an experience. Greco did not speak English very well just then, and I was not sure at all if he clearly understood what I was saying to him, nor about Rolf's idea that we should produce and publish a book together on the Wing Chun art. Rolf was very enthusiastic about the prospect whilst I was thinking about whether I would even get the money back which would have to be invested in the book.

The book grew, by degrees, and then one day Rolf and I set out to the suburbs of London where Greco lived, to meet him again and take photographs to be used in the work, which was to be called "Wing Chun Kung Fu". Little did I realise to what extent Greco was dubious about doing the book at all. He was steeped in the Chinese tradition that no foreigners should be shown Chinese Kung Fu. It was firmly believed that the secrets of the arts, whatever their effectiveness, should be closely guarded and it was unthinkable to break this code.

Across the Atlantic it was already being broken to some extent, and certainly there were foreigners who knew something of Kung Fu, even then. But they were a tiny, tiny minority. I hope that I give no offence to Greco Wong, whom I have not seen for decades now, when I say that we had almost to lure him out of his flat and into the garden. To me, a westerner, it was hard to comprehend why anyone should be so nervous about having his picture taken, and why the Chinese felt so deeply about revealing their arts. Be that as it may, Greco appeared in the garden from behind the house wall, as if someone were waiting to hit him with a club.

Slowly we got the pictures we wanted, with Greco hesitating every minute, wondering if we should show this technique or that technique, and had we already revealed more than we should, and so on... The book showed some moves which are now commonplace, and the first level Set of Wing Chun, Siu Lim Tao, or Little Idea. The book was published. There was no lightning strike from Hong Kong, and no sudden acclaim from the relatively benighted English martial artists. The latter reaction was to come later.

As editor of K.O.A. I received the occasional guarded phone call from person or persons often unknown, stressing to me that Wing Chun was a guarded style, and that no Chinese would ever reveal the "true secrets". I did not know what to make of all this then. It seemed to me that somewhere there was a hidden network of communicating Sinophiles, all whispering together about the secrets of Kung Fu, and that they directed some of their decisions in my direction for reasons best known to themselves. Was I being threatened, I wondered, but Rolf reassured me that it was o.k. and that the book had not been condemned by "them".

Eventually Greco moved to Africa, and then to Canada. I received the occasional Christmas card from him, and then silence. I believe that Rolf too did

Greco Wong poses for a side view of a basic Wing Chun hand position.

emigrate and we lost touch. At the point of our meeting, we were all three too inexperienced to take advantage of what lay ahead... Bruce Lee.

When Bruce Lee died and "Enter the Dragon" appeared, thousands of people in the martial arts world, and hundreds of thousands of would-be martial artists, went mad. An English publishing company wanted to produce a martial arts one-off publication all about Bruce and they wanted to advertise books in the publication, FREE! They asked me if I had anything suitable; I said I had, and "Wing Chun Kung Fu" was one of the books chosen. The publication came out, and we sold a few...

"Time Out" magazine also wanted books to write about, there were not many on Kung Fu around then, and they also featured our books, FREE! Believe it or not, most of our company's income from these book sales was used to prop up K.O.A. magazine, which was finding it hard to get enough advertising revenue, which is the lifeblood of magazine publishing. We owe Bruce Lee for that, at least.

Not unsurprisingly, martial arts teachers were not slow to jump on the band wagon. How can you resist when the public is lining up outside your door to pay for lessons and membership at your club. It did not matter, for 99% of the customers, whether you were teaching Karate, Aikido, Jujitsu or what. People just wanted to put on a uniform, punch and kick the air, shout and do something oriental-martial. Others wanted to know how Bruce Lee did so well, who had taught him, what was his style, and so on. When it leaked out that one of his first loves in martial arts had been Wing Chun, the cat was out of the bag. Wing Chun instructors, good, bad and indifferent, were able to

Derek Jones was a British Wing Chun enthusiast. He came to see me as editor of K.O.A. to ask if I could help him with his plans. Originally he learned from Sifu Victor Kan, and then opened his own school not very far from K.O.A. offices, in the Shepherds Bush area of West London. He was youthful, strong and full of energy. From time to time pupils of his would come to the shop and speak highly of him. Characteristically of many martial arts young men, Derek urgently wished to convince you of something. You listened, probably agreed, and then wondered where do we go from here?

In Derek's case you went into films. He brought me a video short of himself performing martial arts. Someone had charged him a lot of money for making this promotional tape. We talked, and I pointed out that K.O.A. was not a big time magazine and appearing in it would not do much to help him break into the film industry. He really needed a good showbiz agent.

I heard from him from time to time. A private pupil of his came to see me, questioning me about martial arts. I later heard that this man was writing his own book, but I did not realise it then. I guardedly said that I had never seen Derek Jones in action so my views would not be particularly useful. Then, news came through that Derek had died in a motorbike accident. His pupils were shocked. He might have gone on to great things.

It occurred to me that like the man he had admired, Bruce Lee, Derek Jones had also passed away before he was able to realise his own dreams and aspirations.

command very high prices for teaching the art and they did so. And why not? It was a simple case of supply and demand.

Among the teachers to emerge, and the list is not exhaustive by any means, were William Cheung, Leung Ting, Victor Kan, Samuel Kwok, Simon Lau, Doug Wong, Augustine Fong, Dunn Wah and Joseph Cheng. Later some western pupils, for instance Alan Lamb and Nino Bernardo began to teach. Incidentally, what financial arrangements these named teachers had with their pupils, I do not know, nor am I associating them in any way with the remarks in the previous paragraph.

Hard on the heels of the Bruce Lee boom and the lesser Wing Chun explosion came a hailstorm of controversy within the ranks of the Wing Chun fraternity. It is probably something they would prefer to forget but it needs to be mentioned to give a more rounded picture. There was a lot of money, some serious money, to be made in teaching in those days. Not unexpectedly there was competition for pupils. Wing Chun teachers vied with one another to prove that they were either teaching the best, original, traditional style of Wing Chun or that they had been the closest to Grandmaster Yip Man or at least that they had spent the longest time studying. Some teachers even sent their pupils to challenge other Wing Chun stylists or pupils of other styles, to show theirs was the most effective method. It was all very sad and in a sense predictable, and let's face it, understandable.

karate

AND ORIENTAL ARTS   75p   FEB./MAR. 1984   No. 106

VICTOR KAN'S
WING CHUN
TRADITION

KI CONTROVERSY
CONTINUES

MONKEY STYLE KUNG FU KING
THAI BOXING BATTLERS

A dramatic and eye catching cover shot of Sifu Victor Kan with the Wing Chun knives 'made history' with its background of Big Ben and the Houses of Parliament; rare English sunshine glinting on the steel...

*Below:
Alan Lamb showing a Wing Chun technique with D. Schumaker. Lamb promoted the art in County Durham.*

Note: research conducted by Robert Chu, Rene Ritchie and Y. Wu reveals no less than eight further lineages of Wing Chun styles, and even more in countries such as Vietnam and Malaysia. This information was not available to the martial arts world at large until the middle of this decade - Editor.

The Bruce Lee Input...

As far as I can see, there is little evidence of Bruce Lee's dedication to Wing Chun in his film fight sequences, which are on the whole geared to spectacle. Wing Chun would anyway have been lost on cinema audiences. It is too fast and too subtle for the feature film screen. It is also said that when Lee went to the U.S.A. and met martial artists maybe a foot taller than he was and nearly twice his weight, he realised the need for powerful kicks; fists were not enough.

However, this does not detract from the value of Wing Chun, nor from the store Bruce Lee set by it in his teachings and notes. In the writings which have been published, it is clear that the principles of Wing Chun remained in the background of his martial arts thinking like a sentinel. When he writes about boxing for instance this is obvious:

> "Always follow up and press your advantage after countering until the opponent goes down or fights back."

and,

> "Conditioned action should be the result of intense and concentrated practice of planned action patterns in response to every lead."

This advice, from *The Tao of Jeet Kune Do* is typical of Wing Chun training methods and conditioning, or Set practice.

Young martial artists of today cannot imagine how poor, compared with the standards of today, the level of martial arts kicking techniques were some twenty-five to thirty years ago. To begin with, kicking had never been a western mode of fighting, apart from Savate or Boxe Francaise. People had for the most part experienced punching from the boxing influence, and a much smaller number had some Judo experience. Leaving aside thugs and commando trained ex-army men, the very joints used in kicking had lain neglected in the loins of the population!

As Karate and then Taekwondo spread, the kicking habit grew, but it was very limited. Few people had studied exactly how kicking was done, and the books devoted to kicking and stretching had not appeared. It was the pressure of the film business, initially led by Bruce Lee's successes, that opened up a whole new kicking game. People wanted to be able to kick, spin and kick, leap and kick, leap and double kick in the air. What appeared on screen had to appear in the training halls, and the media influence pulled the cash out of the bag to make it all happen. Today it is not difficult to find a martial artist who can kick almost as fast as he or she can punch! When Bruce Lee showed on screen how he could manoeuvre himself round in a circle on one leg and be able to kick, keeping his balance, the martial arts fans wanted to be able to do it too.

Slowly, the big division between the less realistic Lee enthusiasts who wanted to be like Bruce was on film, and the more canny enthusiasts who realised that there was something deeper behind the star's public image, grew. The media on the whole, were sceptical about this and had for the most part a derisory attitude. At one Karate press conference I attended, they more or less insulted the experts present; the latter kept their cool, almost, and stalked off. Reporters and photographers little realised how close they had come to sampling the art they viewed with such bad mannered incredulity. This was counterbalanced some time later at another such conference when Chinese Wushu experts bent spears to breaking point using their necks.

So Bruce Lee's close pupils continued his ideas, moving from Wing Chun and the methods of Escrima, into Jun Fan, and later taking in other methods of fighting and putting them under the Jeet Kune Do microscope. As always happens, divisions appeared in even this group. Some remained tied as it were to the first ideas and methods, whilst others moved on, finding in Lee's message the inspiration to experiment, find what works and adapt it into one's own understanding of what martial arts is all about.

These latter were justified, when a South American form of Jujutsu began to sweep all opposition aside in the early part of this decade. Taking on all-comers, the Jujutsu experts proved, so it seemed to eye witnesses, that a good grappler-wrestler could beat anyone. People who lived in the world of wrestling or who knew wrestlers had sometimes said this to me, but I had no experience to go on. I just knew from looking at them, that wrestlers were very dangerous people.

In England for instance, Bob Breen, a dedicated martial artist and close pupil of Dan Inosanto, said in an interview in *Combat* magazine, May 1998:

> The orginal Jun Fan was great but what Bruce was doing was for
> the sixties, when everyone was doing karate. Everybody has moved
> on now. Now there are pentjak silat(from southeast Asia and Indo-
> nesia), Thai boxing, shoot wrestling and Brazilian jiu jitsu...

> ...Some people think that JKD is a bit of this and a bit of that. Well,
> no, it's not! It's understanding a core, whether it's boxing, judo,
> kickboxing or Thai, and saying, "What are the deficiencies of this style?

Sifu Jospeh Cheng wrote a book for us, and this was previewed in KOA no. 70 in 1978.

CHONG WOO KWAN WING CHUN

Joseph Cheng shows preview of new textbook

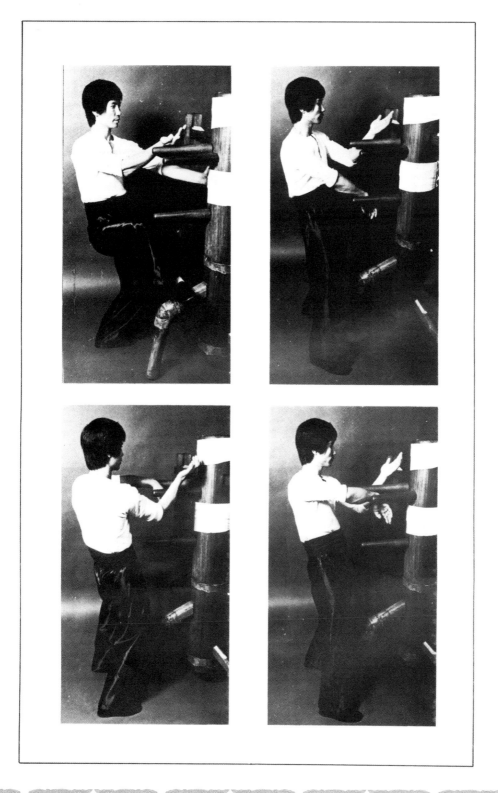

"O.K., I can be trapped or tied up by a person who's got good sensitivity skills, so I need to understand the sensitivity skills in order that I can counteract them."

In saying this, the experienced and very dedicated Bob Breen said something which should be a guide for all would-be JKD students as well as the ones who are already in training. What Bob did not say, because it was not part of the interview, was that he and others like him have decades of martial arts experience behind them. When you have trained hard for a long time, with intelligence and a critical mind, you develop a nose for things in the field. You can look at another martial artist from another style, and if he is truly showing his own thing, and not trying to pull the wool over your eyes, you can pick up something about him, or her, which comes only from this "nose".

He may make only a few moves, but you catch something deep and fundamental about his art. This was probably one of the reasons why martial artists from the East would not show anything they wanted to keep to themselves. They knew about this "nose" and how sensitive it can become. They did not want others to "suss them out" so they kept their art under wraps to be able to use it, with all its surprises, when the time came. This is part of what Bob Breen was talking about. But it is rare for a youngster, or someone who has not given dedication to an art, to be able to do this. So, as the interview pointed out, JKD is not a style as such, but an attitude towards training which is a kind of quest, supported by hard work and experience. It is not a passport to instant skill based on the mistaken notion that you need not train at any particular style.

At the same time, there is one fact which not exactly goes against the JKD ideal but makes it hard to realise. This is the fact that every martial artist is marked or conditioned by the first style he studied. If he is originally a boxer it will be boxing, if karate then karate, if Wing Chun then Wing Chun. To make over all the reflexes and conditionings of that first strong hard training may be beyond most people. It would require a great deal of energy, and/or probably a very special genetic inheritance. After all, it was that first left jab, performed twenty thousand or forty thousand times, which kept you out of trouble for years, so how hard it must be to put it on one side and rely on grappling, or on specialized praying mantis punching or aikido locking and throwing. Even harder it must be to have them all at your finger-tips and when the occasion demands make a split second, subconscious choice to use the most appropriate action from a range of styles you have studied.

The JKD ideal implies such a situation and such a capacity. My own view, from the outside of course, is that Bruce Lee was so to speak "marked" by

Wing Chun. There is something about this art which creeps through his writings and movements. Wing Chun can be seen as a "frozen" style, with traditions which should not be changed or developed. On the other hand, it can be seen as a really excellent basis for development, using its straight line theory and deflecting-parrying methods as fundamental to that development. After all, the Forms or Sets, their content, are nothing more and nothing less than an interpretation of fundamentals. In actual combat, the Sets themselves are in a sense lost to the requirements of a situation. The movements of the Sets make an assumption that you will be attacked in such and such a way, but this is a limited view. You do not know how you will be attacked. You do not know if the attack will come from another Wing Chun expert or a street fighter with no "method" or someone crazy from drugs use, temporarily oblivious to pain.

With this in mind, the JKD ideal is what comes to the rescue. Someone said, "Be prepared, but be ready to improvise," and it wasn't the Boy Scouts, either of the Baden-Powell or Bruce Willis varieties! So, JKD is really for the truly dedicated martial artist who is not interested in perfecting a style, but in perfecting his own readiness to cope with any situation. It opens up the way for the widest possible study into human anatomy, physiology, philosophy, religion and many other things which Bruce Lee, if one dare say so, was mentally facing when he passed away. He did not leave, to my knowledge, any coherent and organised written statement of his search. He "spoke" best when he moved, when he was teaching live, when he was spontaneous. Maybe, if he had lived long enough, and continued in his quest, he would have eventually produced such a statement either in words or film. We shall never know.

Meanwhile, standard bearers such as Bob Breen, James DeMile, Jesse Glover, Dan Inosanto, Richard Bustillo and the rest continue to search and research in ways which Lee himself might have done. The difficulty here is that such people may go so far into the distance that they leave the majority of martial artists behind, and become able to be understood only by people following on who have the same search, the same unquenchable desire to keep the ideal alive. This is not only inevitable but in my view it is the right and acceptable situation, the just situation.

DAN INOSANTO

The best known pupil, friend, and in some respects teacher of Bruce Lee is Dan Inosanto. It was Inosanto who introduced Lee to Escrima, or Filipino martial arts. Inosanto acknowledges Bruce Lee's indebtedness to Wing Chun, and portrays it as the basis for Lee's "art" of Jun Fan, the name he gave the methods and thoughts he had come to in the early 1960's. Inosanto briefly analysed Wing Chun down to its bare bones, in his own book, "Jeet Kune Do - the Art and Philosophy of Bruce Lee", and concluded this analysis by saying:

> In any event, I think it is safe to say that Wing Chun does in fact form the nucleus of Jeet Kune Do. For only with a basic foundation that is already stripped down practically to the essentials could he (Lee) have made such rapid and amazing strides in the development of his own art..."

Inosanto points out that Jun Fan contained also some elements of Northern Chinese kicking methods, since Bruce Lee found that Wing Chun was for him too limited. Dan Inosanto emerges from the years spent with Bruce Lee as the most eloquent of his pupils, who, for the most part, remained less than outspoken, in print, about their mentor. Though carrying the Jeet Kune Do banner high, and continuing to extol the virtues of its philosophy, Inosanto did not hide the fact that he was already a well versed martial artist when he met Lee. Training in judo, jujutsu, Filipino martial arts, and "several styles of Karate" meant that he already had a sturdy framework of methods when the time came. How different this makes him from someone who comes to JKD from an untrained background. Is this "better" or "worse"? In practical terms, in individual instances, it is a superfluous question, because each martial artist is what he is. Better or worse don't matter. But it is the type of question which martial artists love to get their teeth into; it is a question which is a basis for discussion, investigation and learning. The validity of the question does not matter. It is only those who expect a literal answer who come adrift.

In my own experience you can be lightly sparring or playing around, and then suddenly, out of the past, a technique which you learned from Judo, or which someone once showed you from Wing Chun, suddenly pops into your moves at the time. Or, for instance, your partner can throw a jab and you find yourself using the Pull Down move from Tai Chi Chuan. A martial artist discussion might then say, "Oh, well, this sudden inspiration is fine, but someone who had no previous experience might have come up with that move anyway, (or), he might have come up with the same move spontaneously." To which the reply could be, "And then again he might not have..." So it would go on. This free moving approach is the one I associate with Inosanto, a kind of live and let live approach, if it works use it.

Fundamentally, the JKD approach can be summed up by the phrase,

Looking for Mozart...

The boy genius Mozart could compose the most beautiful music and play it almost as soon as he could sit up straight! He aroused jealousy, admiration and amazement. Unlike Lao-tze he was not born old, nor with a background of training at different music academies under different teachers. Bruce Lee had to be trained. The fact is that there are few Mozarts, maybe only one. Ideally the JKD philosophy is to be like Mozart, drawing upon something which goes beyond description, beyond training and if the truth be told beyond common human understanding. This means it truly is an *ideal,* because such a thing is virtually impossible.

Everyone in the martial arts world who is anyone has trained, has followed the "classical mess" and been strengthened and tuned by it. This means that such individuals have something to draw upon when they cannot find the "Mozart touch".   "Make a plan but be prepared to impovise", and such is the case here. Behind the discussion and controversy about JKD, and what it implies, is the subject of the basic human being and how he or she is constructed, and what is the potential therein.

Classical Chinese martial arts theory has approached this theme when it refers to different types of energy: listening energy, sensitivity energy, and so forth. These energies are not available at the touch of a button. They are dependent on certain internal relationships which in turn are dependent on certain disciplines and methods of training. Talent is not enough. Mozart did not have talent, he had genius, maybe more. He apparently did not need training, and could work at the touch of a button.

For the rest of us, we need to be trained, however spontaneous our future actions may be. I have written elsewhere about a BBC report in which the famous jazz trumpet player Dizzie Gillespie admitted that he very rarely was truly spontaneous. This was an honest and remarkable admission from such a man. It means that however brilliantly he played he was in fact for a lot of the time drawing on memory in a way which was recognisable to him when he played "improvised" jazz music. I cite it, in drawing this section to a close, just to add fuel to the JKD flame. Bruce Lee, and Dan Inosanto, produced and maintained such ideas, and thereby they both enriched the martial arts world. But without Wing Chun, without Grandmaster Yip Man, what would they have done? Linda Lee wrote that Yip Man's Wing Chun "inspired Bruce to do his greatest work." There you have it.

Where some of the more outspoken traditionalists in Chinese martial arts have come badly unstuck is in making claims about what they can do. One memorable instance in more recent years was the Empty Force incident.

A Scottish Tai Chi instructor, Dan Docherty, became involved in this affair because he believed that a martial artist should put his money where his mouth is. He had earlier challenged a Chinese Tai Chi expert to a Push Hands contest and uprooted him, and when another expert claimed he could push people over and affect inanimate objects such as water with this same Empty Force, Docherty was curious. He travelled to meet this unusual expert, approached him and poured water over him. The expert was not able to push the water away... A famous Wing Chun expert was lured into a situation he knew nothing about, and floored by a Turkish wrestler, much to the dismay of his students, not to mention his own. In the 1970's the controversial Hungarian self defence teacher, Lajos Jakab, resident in London, England, regularly visited Sifu who claimed that they were expert fighters and proved otherwise. Though Lajos Jakab caused a lot of ill-feeling, he was also very popular, and was always willing to take on any challenge himself. There are no doubt dozens of stories of this type where a martial artist has over-stepped the mark and been shown up.

On the other side of the coin, I have heard of Americans going to Taiwan and China, challenging Chinese traditionalists and being badly beaten. One such was a man who studied Pakua who took on a Hsing-I expert and got severely punished. The lesson that claimants to invincibility or unusual powers could learn from Bruce Lee's JKD is the well known one of if it works, use it, and if it does not, discard it. There can be no sacred combat cows in martial arts. Another lesson is that you never know whom you are facing. The most harmless looking person may be absolutely deadly, and the big, muscular braggart may be useless. A third lesson is one that I heard from a merchant seaman who had seen lots of fighting in his day, which was that in a real fight the first punch is the last one; not always true, of course, but it underlines Jack Dempsey's words (World Heavyweight Champion boxer) to the effect that the longer a fight goes on the more chance there is of being hurt, so learn to win with one punch.

So leaving all philosophy and debate aside, what JKD can also be said to offer is practical common sense in combat. Finish the fight in the best way possible. Style does not count in this. Take the currently unbeaten boxer, Prince Naseem. Did any boxer every fight the way he does? He breaks all the classic rules of the noble art of pugilism yet wins. He moves more like a lightweight wrestler than a boxer, and punches from nowhere. It must really get up the noses of many traditional trainers and boxers alike, but they cannot deny the results of his fights. Likewise, Bruce Lee got up the noses of many traditionalists in his field, yet no one ever defeated him, though many wished to do so. The most candid statements of Bruce Lee's motivation and methods have come from James DeMile, as far as my own research goes, and they can be summed up in a few words: Bruce Lee wanted to win.

The Filipino Connection

One of Bruce Lee's close friends, who was also his teacher and pupil, was Dan Inosanto. Dan was steeped in the Filipino arts of stick, knife and empty hand combats. Dan took up JKD and Bruce was very interested in the stick as a fighting weapon; see "Enter the Dragon"...

Arnis de Mano, Kali, Escrima are three of the names used to describe a class of fighting techniques espoused by Dan Inosanto and his friends. The techniques are used by the martial artists of the Filipino fraternities or Escrimadores. In 1975 a now famous, but then less well known teacher of Escrima

Escrimador

*

Rene Latosa

called Rene Latosa came to England. One of his first ports of call was the KOA office, as he naturally wanted some magazine publicity and we were happy to oblige. As often happened in such circumstances, Rene showed me the basics of his art and as I imitated his moves I was duly impressed.

Some key

elements of the

Filipino arts are...

pattern,

fluidity,

improvisation,

agility,

speed.

During the wave of publicity which followed Bruce Lee's death and accompanied the distribution of "Enter the Dragon", the Filipino connection was hardly mentioned in the popular press, or press releases. The fact that Bruce Lee used a pair of sticks in the penultimate fight scenes against Han's henchmen did not get much emphasis.

His nunchaku or "rice flails", later to become notorious, were eventually banned by the British government and some States of the United States. They were much more appealing to his young fans than sticks. In addition, a different style of nunchaku was already in use in Japanese and Okinawan karate so that teachers of this method were already around.

Until Rene Latosa and later Dan Inosanto put in an appearance in England, the Filipino stick arts were a closed book over here. On the West Coast of the U.S.A. and elsewhere, communities of Filipinos existed and some of their members were skilled in the art. Prominent among the English martial artists who were attracted to Escrima was Bill Newman, a Londoner, who was also interested in boxing and later in Jeet Kune Do concepts and methods. In those days, English martial artists were still very ingenuous in their field. Even when they had become acquainted with the stick fighting methods, they had for the most part to be told that the stick could be a substitute for a long blade.

Nowadays, there are many martial artists who are so to speak very sophisticated, and see immediately that an empty hand art can be converted to a weapons art, and vice-versa, and that the use of one weapon can be converted into another without too much trouble, provided you have some skill in one of them. It goes without saying that Bruce Lee already had that adaptive skill and would have had no problem in converting freely from weapon to weapon . Indeed his writings indicate that this was the case. It was part of his fundamental concept that if sufficient spontaneous skill is part of a martial artist's make-up then he will be able to adapt to any situation.

Some of the key elements of the Filipino arts are:

pattern - fluidity of movement - improvisation - agility - speed

In my few lessons with Rene Latosa I had made the mistake of thinking of the Escrima sticks as clubs, and that the targets for attack and countering would be the head. When I tried this, Rene shook his own head in quiet

Dan Inosanto explaining how very, very simple it all is... *(Photo by Norma Harvey)*

disapproval, as if saying that such a target was far too devastating and that with what in effect was a blade, the wrist or elbow targets would be quite sufficient. It was the intention to disable, not to kill...

One noticeable thing about Rene was that he had "weight". By this I mean that there was a weight in his hands and moves which was very telling, without being heavy. They were the hands of a professional, sure and accurate. I learned the very basic moves of Escrima, filed them away somewhere in the memory bank, and went on with studying Tai Chi, my preferred style at that time. Rene went on to become a well known figure in Europe and the United States and is still teaching, assisted in Europe by Bill Newman.

Dan Inosanto

Dan Inosanto was a very different person. He has been in films playing bit parts, displaying his martial skills; but as Bruce Lee's fame spread so did his. I went on two seminars that he gave in London, and one could see the knowledge and ability oozing out of him. It was more than anyone could take in at one time, and all I can say is that I picked up certain impressions of him, and his laid back style of moving, which were more useful than specific technical points.

What happened as Escrima and Jeet Kune Do gathered martial arts momentum is that they began to be analysed, formalised and almost ritualised. Many of the martial arts methods which Bruce Lee had written and taught about appeared in the JKD "curriculum". Book after book appeared, devoted to this or that aspect of JKD and a number of books on Escrima and related arts accompanied them. In a sense, this was nothing more nor less than a response to the public demand for information and instruction. The "Do" or Way of JKD would have required intense dedication, and the majority of fans and devotees were not capable of that.

During the martial arts boom, the B.B.C. television put on a panoramic series of programmes called "The Way of the Warrior" which featured martial arts from around the world. A very interesting programme was devoted to Escrima centred around indigenous teachers. In this programme it was clear that there was the old, naturally developed Escrima and the formalised teaching methods which were gaining in popularity. Every now and then one glimpsed the deadly, unscheduled flashes of technical skill, like the strike of the cobra, and it was clear that Escrima, like Japanese swordsmanship, was rooted in a social situation, not in a western oriented semi-recreational one.

Bruce
Lee's
ability
to analyse
his
opponents'
attacks,
to know
the moves
they would
make
before
they
made them
was startling.

*(Dan
Inosanto)*

Dan Inosanto continued to visit Britain, and other Englishmen surfaced as keen followers of the ideas and methods he promoted. Among these were Mark Romain, Nino Bernardo and Bob Breen. The latter gradually devoted much of his life to these arts, branching out into the study of other uses of weapons from other eastern countries. However, Inosanto remained for many students the fountainhead of knowledge and tuition.

He was sometimes assisted by Richard Bustillo, another of Bruce Lee's students. A report in KOA magazine in the May/June 1980 edition from a seminar Dan had given in Ontario under the auspices of the Canadian Jujitsu Assocation at the Oakland Regional Centre read:

> "The totality and combat efficiency of JKD was clearly visiible in the explosive hand strikes, the economy of motion, the fluidity, lightning parries and simple hand traps.

> "During the period after the seminar, Dan Inosanto and Richard Bustillo answered many questions concerning some traditional concepts, techniques and training methods. When questioned about Bruce Lee's phenomenal fighting ability, Dan Inosanto put it this way: 'Bruce Lee had tremendous speed, strength and natural fighting ability. He trained many hours every day... but his asets were his extraordinary perception and sensitivity. His ability to analyse his opponent's attacks, to know the moves they would make before they made them was startling.' "

Though Dan Inosanto's own abilities as an all round martial artist is great, he has always been associated with the movie star who died and left him with a name, Jeet Kune Do, which has overshadowed everything else. One suspects however that those close to Inosanto understand the true proportion or allocation of understanding in the matter. Inosanto is a martial artist in his own right; though he owes his fame to Bruce Lee, his understanding is his own.

His martial arts forebears, the peoples of the Phillipines, were conquered by the Spanish. The invaders forbade the use of martial arts weapons, blades, and outlawed training in the methods. But by using sticks and empty hands, perhaps like the Okinawans under Japanese rule, they kept their arts alive and by necessity secret. Tough, enduring and subtle, the Filipinos did not need Jeet Kune Do to survive. This is the practical reality which should be the basis for viewing Bruce Lee in relation to Escrima and the Escrimadores.

Early days... It is autumn 1975, a young American airman Rene Latosa is about to make a big impact in London, England. He is shown patiently explaining technical points of Escrima on Putney Heath, not far from K.O.A. office, to a young James Shortt, then a Jujutsu specialist, and a not quite so young Paul Crompton.

Latrosa has parried another attack and his hand depresses Shortt's hand whilst the stick rotates to attack the wrist. Many old time 'escrimadores' attacked the wrist aiming to disarm and not kill or seriously injure. Pay attention too to the 'clamping action of the stick and hand together

Latrosa explains to Shortt the parry action of the stick followed by a depressing action of the hand, making sure the partner cannot continue his attack. Notice that he uses hand on hand, so the parry could be used to block a knife thrust too. In that case a sharp flick would be employed.

Latrosa shows Shortt the 'safest' place to put the hand if using it to supplement the parry of the stick.

Shortt gets a sharp lesson with a wooden sword, in long distance play. The wrist again is the focal point.

Latosa shows Crompton how to make an opening for the stick by using the empty hand.

Crompton demonstrates the direction of the strike.

Latrosa shows stick parry to be followed by a hand block.

Latrosa continues his turn at the waist and shows a typical strike

Among the "grand old men" or masters of Filipino arts to appear to the public gaze were Porfirio Lanada and Angel Cabales. They were both reluctant to reveal and see revealed the secret fighting arts of their country, but when they realised that an irresistible force of interest was driving aside all considerations of authenticity, and that confectioned styles of Escrima were leaping up on all sides, they acquiesced and their arts were published. They thought it better that something approaching the real thing be available rather than the public be misled by self-appointed teachers.

The style of Porfirio Lanada is called Arnis Lanada, and that of Angel Cabales is known as Cabales Serrada Escrima. As the Filipino arts were revealed, students learned that there were many more than they had imagined, scattered throughout the archipelago. The parallel with Okinawa was fascinating. The northern style best known in the West is called Arnis de Mano, in the centre of the country it is Escrima and in the south, Kali. As western students probed further into the history and development of these arts it became a clear that this history was steeped in blood. Filipino Escrimadores had reputations based not on boasting, boxing ring knock-outs or newspaper headlines, but on actual fights to the death. This information touched a nerve in some western students and they felt that at last they had found something which was truly authentic. It was based on what worked, and as such was kin to Bruce Lee's own views. Fortunately, the Filipino teachers had their own methods of judging whether a pupil merited being taught, and this was a sure fire safety gate for keeping out hooligans. A national hierarchy of standards was mainatined, with only the best of the best being admitted to the Doce Pares Society.

Everyone knows from television that the famed Shaolin temple of "Kung Fu - Carradine" programmes that there were a series of tests which a trainee monk had to undergo. One of these tests was to pass along a gauntlet of wooden figures which struck out at the novice and which he had to block, duck and dodge. In the Doce Pares tradition, there is an account of a similar gauntlet, consisting of weapons triggered by foot pressure. One famous Escrimador had the distinction of being the only man to emerge from this tunnel unscathed. His name was Felicisimo Dizon. Angel Cabales was his pupil. He eventually found his way to the United States, and taught there until his death in 1991. Among his pupils were Dan Inosanto, Richard Bustillo and Rene Latosa. Thus, over a long period, a martial art from a distant, little appreciated country and fostered by a relatively unknown teacher, Felicisimo Dizon, found its way, however modified the form, into the film "Enter the Dragon", and into the eyes of many millions of people the world over. The Filipino connection was made.

Below is the first Escrima story to appear in Britain, in KOA no. 57, November 1975

No uniforms? No elaborate ceremonial? No bows to an opponent whom you may or may not respect? That's right, none. . . The Filipino art of Escrima, or Kali, or Arnis de Mano concentrates on a man's ability to use the stick. It's split second arm-jarring parries and lightning follow through that counts. Escrimadores is the name given to those who study Escrima. A man who is entitled to call himself an 'escrimador' is Rene Latosa of California, who was recently interviewed by Seamus Shortt and Paul Crompton. Not only did his stick art impress but he came armed with recommendations from the Virginia Police Training Department, Richard S. Bustillo, Angel Cabales of the Stockton Escrima Academy, Dan Revillar of the Sacramento Escrima Academy and last of all Dan Inosanto President of the Jeet Kane Do Jun Fan Gung Fu Institute of California. Here's his story.

Latosa had had a number of instructors in Escrima and was quite skilled when he approached his own father, a man in his sixties. He asked the senior member of the family to test his skill. Needless to say, Rene had never tried his father's skill with a stick before. He didn't recall ever seeing the "old man" touch one, but the moment of truth came. Never strike till he commits himself, is the motto of an escrimador. Latosa's father watched, and watched. Latosa, knowing many techniques, feinted, gave a few uncompleted attacks but his father wasn't convinced. As soon as the real one came, Latosa found himself defeated. With unerring hand and eye Latosa senior struck.

Rene recalls: "I couldn't touch him. I knew I still had to learn what escrima was about." This experience underlines a traditional side of Filipino people. In the words of Teodoro A. Agoncillo (A Short History of the Philippines),
"Respect for elders is an important Filipino trait. Filipino parents do not condone children talking back to their elders." Latosa has good reason to remember that.

As seen in the traditions of the Philippines escrima has a sound basis. An older, weaker, family member does not find himself at a disadvantage in the art. Strong, wild and impulsive youth can be outwitted and outfought by experience, timing and calmness. Strength does not play a leading part. You can be as strong as a bull but your muscle power is no use to you without other qualities.

Ferdinand Magellan, a sixteenth century Portuguese explorer, was commissioned to try to improve the spice trade and "edge out the Venetians" who had a strong control in that field. After numerous adventures and a crew that almost mutinied he arrived at the Marianas. The first Spanish-sponsored landing was thus made in the Philippines in March, 1521.

A Catholic mass was said and on the same island, Limasawa, Magellan made a blood compact with a native chief. Sailing on he came to Cebu and persuaded 800 native Filipinos to become Christian, and be baptised. But Magllan's fate was sealed when he became involved in the small wars of the native chiefs and he was killed. The natives of Cebu were "disenchanted" with the Spanish and massacred the whole contingent on the sea shore. During the following centuries Spain took control of the Philippines until it was finally taken over by the Americans and later in modern times became independent.

Everyone knows by now the story that the weapon arts of Okinawa were given an extra jolt by the edict against the carrying of conventional weapons. Likewise when the Spanish invaders saw a performance of escrima they forbade it. It is important to bear in mind that escrima can also be done with swords and with knives and with empty hands.

But, the Spaniards did not know that like other martial arts escrima is also 'hidden' in some of the traditional dances of the Philippines. Visitors even today in search of a deadly' art can be disappointed when they are shown only a harmless looking dance instead of the true fighting escrima in application

The Spaniards were deceived. Escrima flourished in secret and in secret it flourished before their admiring and unsuspecting eyes.

During the centuries of Filipino troubles, the stick art has been there to give its aid. When the U.S.A. began to encourage immigration, the Filipinos took escrima with them. It was during the Bruce Lee boom that Dan Inosanto showed the art on the screen, and since that time it has been growing in popularity. Many of the original immigrants are very old or they have died. It is the aim of the present generation of escrimadores to preserve and cultivate the traditions and to explore more fully the potentialities of the systems; 'systems' because there are many.

"No one can lay down a hard line about it", commented Latosa, "but when I see those X-blocks shown to stop a knife," he shook his head, "I wonder." Seamus Shortt imitated a knife thrust and Latosa blocked with an X. What happened was bad for his wrists, and Shortt did not have to have it explained to him, why Latosa's X-block was a danger to himself.

When Latosa taught in the U.S.A. he chose his pupils. "You can't just take anybody. Escrima is for serious students. Sometimes people I know who do martial arts say, 'C'mon stop this,' and throw a punch or a kick. I just step out of the way. With a stick you have to be careful. Someone who doesn't know them can be injured just by his own ignorance. I'm not saying stick escrima is better than empty hands, believe me. It's just that you need to have tried them before you judge them."

Escrima rarely uses double handed techniques. The emphasis is on speed. Some Japanese methods employ both hands, in particular this is shown where a stick is used to trap or throw an opponent. Such techniques are useful in stopping a man from continuing to struggle, as in police work, which is where several Japanese weapons arts have been studied in modern times. Footwork is simple and direct in escrima too, and shows none of the large varieties in stance which occupy the repertoire of Chinese, Japanese and Okinawan styles of combat. The basic pattern for footwork is a triangle with the two feet moving between the three points.

Like Filipino hospitality escrima demands a kind of patience. It goes without saying that a guest is as welcome as long as he wants to stay. The approach of escrima is 'submissive' in the sense that an escrimador waits. He submits until the last minute, until the attacker has really committed himself and then counters with speed and precision. Thus his 'submissiveness' helps him to overcome.

Latosa himself is modest and self-effacing, and not over-talkative. Unlike some of our American brothers in the martial arts he lets actions speak louder than words. He would like to see escrima preserved and cultivated in Britain.

There is much more than you might think to this relatively unknown Filipino art. It has none of the outward dignity of Japanese Budo but has a dignity in its very simplicity and efficiency. It is outside the scope of this article to go into detail. Broadly speaking there are systems of escrima, arnis de mano or kali in every region of the Philippines, which at a rough guess has about 10, 000 islands. 'Largo mano' uses a long distance method, and there are techniques for medium and short distances. Regional techniques were kept secret so that enemies from other parts could be taken by surprise during a 'duel.'

"Control is needed," said Latosa. "For instance, when you stop a strike in training, you must know that there is backlash. You can hit yourself if you aren't careful." He demonstrated and the stick vibrated back and forth as he put a stop on it. "Beginners have to appreciate that." Latosa has taught a few basics in London already as guest of Paul Crompton's Tai Chi class. He hopes to be able to extend this instruction to other clubs who are interested as soon as possible.

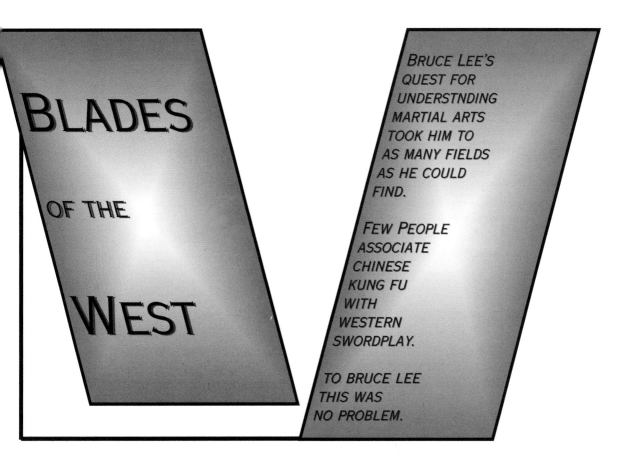

BLADES OF THE WEST

BRUCE LEE'S QUEST FOR UNDERSTNDING MARTIAL ARTS TOOK HIM TO AS MANY FIELDS AS HE COULD FIND.

FEW PEOPLE ASSOCIATE CHINESE KUNG FU WITH WESTERN SWORDPLAY.

TO BRUCE LEE THIS WAS NO PROBLEM.

When most people think of western swordplay, if they are old enough they remember film star Errol Flynn, of "Robin Hood" and "Captain Blood" fame, or if they are younger they recall the intense final duel in the film "Rob Roy", or the sword epic, "The Duellists". The simple truth is that unless you have studied the development of swordsmanship in Europe your imagination takes you little further than films and some vague recollections about swords from school days. We hazily recall that once knights in armour had very big broadswords and later on people used rapiers instead, for some reason, we are not quite clear about, maybe something to do with the invention of firearms.

Let's face it, we're ignorant about the subject!

The fact is that swordplay in Europe was studied and developed every bit as intensively as it was in Japan or China or anywhere else. Men's lives and honour depended on swords, and people were every bit as serious about staying alive in the West as they were in the East. Old books and the remnants of schools of swordsmanship survive to this day to testify to the truth of this.

Though Bruce Lee wrote mainly about empty hand combat the vocabulary he used at times shows his interest in fencing. In "The Tao of Jeet Kune Do" he introduces the word "riposte" which is an expression as a rule never used in martial arts literature for empty hand techniques. He defines it as:

"A riposte is an attack (or more accurately a counterattack) following a parry."

"Parry" too of course is more of a fencing than empty hand term. He goes on to describe methods of parrying, slipping under and around an opponent's attacking arm in ways which belong in a description of rapier or foil techniques. Words like "disengagement, counter disengagement, cut over, feint, sixte" and so forth, call to mind western swordsmanship, so Lee clearly had this art in mind as he was making the relevant notes on his thoughts about fighting. Of all the Chinese empty hand arts I have come across, Wing Chun resembles the methods of western rapier sword play more than any other. It may well have been this similarity which struck Bruce Lee and caused him to devote time and effort to the study of the foreign methods.

Western swordplay is every bit as aware of the centre line as the Wing Chun art.

An important aspect of foil fencing for instance known to all students and noted by Lee is the economy of movement employed. Large, cinematically appealing strokes are counter productive. They leave you open to attack and are a waste of energy. By development of the wrist and also the elbow and shoulder, the *necessary* techniques can be produced around a narrow centre-line, only moving outwards to a limit of the outline of the body. This is pure Wing Chun.

When a student begins to learn Wing Chun or the western foil, he is bound at first to make movements which are too big. He cannot see that economy is a practical requirement, not a piece of artificially introduced limitation. The result is primary, that is, to make contact or to avoid contact. Everything which leads up to that contact is subservient to it, is designed to produce that result. If you want exercise and exhilaration, you have to find it within the confines of the techniques. So put another way, a beginner does not know where to put his energy, which in the case of a young man or woman is considerable. The discipline is to learn where your energy, your strength, belongs and do the training to be able to bring this about. If you can't, then you should do aerobics instead.

A special feature of K.O.A. in 1980, illustrated by Charles
Hanson, showing methodical study of fencing methods
from old European works.

BRUCE LEE DID NOT LOOK DOWN ON WESTERN METHODS PROVIDED THEY WERE REALLY EFFECTIVE!

We mean no disrespect but some Chinese and Japanese
scoff at systems outside their own culture. This is a mistake.
Usually, Chinese and Japanese who scoff know very little, or
nothing, about Western systems of combat, especially the
older ones.

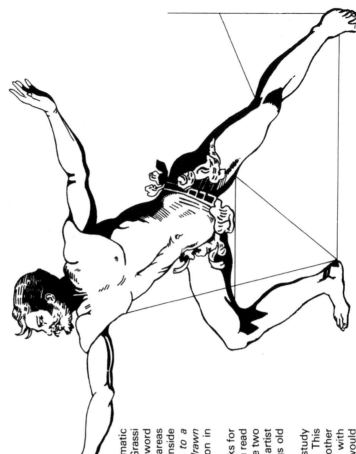

Arthur Wise researched these systems and wrote about them extensively. Bruce Lee was searching for anything in the martial arts field which worked, and he thought very highly of Western fencing. If you have read about Wing Chun Kung Fu, which Bruce learned and made the basis of his Jeet Kune Do, you will appreciate the meaning of indoor and outdoor, centreline and so on. Listen to what Arthur Wise says about 16th century students and teachers of swordplay:

"... both men ... had a logical and systematic approach to the business of personal combat. Grassi further reduced the number of guards with the sword to three ... Grassi ... analysed, too, the four areas in which attacks might be made, as high, low, inside and outside ... *the inside and outside lines lie to a fighter's left and right of an imaginary line drawn vertically through his own body ..."* (and so on in this vein).

Swordplay theory can be transposed to punching attacks for instance and Bruce Lee was not one to miss that. If you read his "Tao Of Jeet Kune Do" you will find references. The two drawings for these pages have been done by our skilled artist to show, by referring to originals, the type of drawings old time writers on swordplay used to convey their ideas.

Another idea which comes into Western writings is the study of the "feel" of another blade during an engagement. This idea comes into Wing Chun and into Tai Chi, and other eastern arts of combat where it is stressed along with technique. A study of these older Western methods would be interesting to all students of martial arts of whatever nationality.

Bruce Lee was not a big man, not a heavy man. He must have realised at an early stage in his combative life that he had to make the very best use of what he had in the way of physical equipment. Grandmaster Yip Man, the father of modern Wing Chun, was also slight, yet his striking power was said to be amazing. Thus, the economies of that art and fencing must have been of tremendous importance to Lee as a youngster. Later, when he began to study martial arts theory, he must have been very gratified to put analytical methods successfully alongside his earlier choice of style.

What follows is a summary of some important facts and theories about western swordplay, drawn from several sources, and a comparison with some of the thoughts written down by Bruce Lee.

Every martial art can give something to the others. No art has everything.

In "Enter the Dragon", Lee at the beginning of a contest rests his wrist against that of his opponent and beats him to the punch. In the 1991 film, "By The Sword", starring Eric Roberts and F. Murray Abraham, a middle aged fencing expert shows a younger champion a method of sensing the pressure of an opponent's blade by an exercise of resting wrist against wrist and attempting to strike through at the face. It is one more example of the similarities between fencing training and empty hand training which attracted Bruce Lee to the subject.

FOIL - In foil fencing the target area is limited to the trunk.

SCORING - To score a point the contestant must use the point of the foil; a hit with the side of the blade is no good.

PARRY - A Parry is made when you deflect your opponent's sword with your own.

RIPOSTE - A Riposte is a counter attack and is permitted after you have made a parry, and your opponent must permit such a riposte.

This means that it is a closely governed type of combat, sometimes compared with tennis, in the sense that *you* hit, and then *I* hit. A thrust to score with the point is like hitting a ball over the net. You wait for the return in the form of a thrust.

LOOKING FOR AN OPENING - Because there are these rule restrictions, time is spent in measuring up your opponent, trying to out-guess him. It is a mixture of mental decisions and physical speed and accuracy.

DISTANCING - It soon becomes clear to a novice fencer that distance is very important. He must be able to judge at what distance he can reach his opponent and what can happen to him when he is within that reach.

ON GUARD - In foil fencing there is a specified on guard position, usually the knees are bent and the foil is presented by an extended sword arm. The on guard position is also related to two other things:

TARGET & DISTANCE: the body target is divided into four areas. The on guard position is related to these areas. The distance is such that if you extended your sword arm you would not be able to strike your opponent without a step forward and lunge.

The on guard position described in the above paragraph is called the **fencing measure.** The on guard position can be with blades touching, **engaged,** or not touching, **absence.** Depending on which part of the body the blades are covering, the guard is said to be **engaged in sixte** for instance.

EMPTY HAND - In the type of combat Bruce Lee was talking about there is no limit on target areas.

SCORING - A score is a hit with any part of the body. It is not a question of a point being awarded but the telling effect of the hit; you 'score' by results.

PARRY - In JKD the emphasis, as in Wing Chun, is to look for methods in which either the parry carries you directly into a counter, or ones in which the parry changes into an attack.

RIPOSTE - The counterattack can be made convention- ally or it can take place even before the attack is com- pleted through the development of anticipation.

Thus, JKD, and its developments, have no rules as such. What works is the accepted "rule". This attitude is simultaneously modern and ancient going back to those found for instance in "The Art of War" and "Book of Five Rings".

OPENINGS - Lee distinguished three methods of prima- ry attack: direct/relying on speed, misleading/using a feint,
power/driving through against all obstacles.

DISTANCING - Lee put forward an interesting but diffi- cult suggestion in connection with this; retreating with diminishing steps to draw an opponent in.

ON GUARD - In his sketches and in other books by Wing Chun teachers, the on guard positions are similar to those of fencing in that they are related to specific areas of the body of the defender.

TARGET & DISTANCE - In JKD and Wing Chun these two factors are so closely inter-connected as to be hard to separate. There are of course no rules about this.

The above elements are too complex to summarise in one para- graph, but the reader can easily see that they are all part of an intricate network of movement, far more complex than that of foil fencing. However, there are also similarities when the movements are artificially isolated and examined.

One art

holds up

the mirror

to another,

especially

when you

are not

blinded by

your own...

K.O.A. no. 59 in 1976 published these two fencing shots, courtesy of "Sword" magazine. We did not know of Lee's interest in swordplay at the time, and the accompanying paragraph about his book appeared above the photos as a pure coincidence.

BRUCE LEE

fans and also serious martial arts men will be glad to see the 'real' Jeet Kune Do book with notes and drawings by the man himself. It is a book to pore over and study. For the serious student it will provide ideas and experiences which can be compared with his own ideas and experiences. Lee does not say "do this", "don't do that", but gives his views for you to try and keep or discard as you think fit. It has been said before but is worth repeating, films and the fast life brought Lee to the top but also robbed the world of a man who could have contributed more, much more, than the pieces of celluloid we have all seen. His book indicates this and perhaps some of his followers will keep his message alive and pass it on to future generations of martial artists.

Below we show glimpses of some exciting moments in recent

fencing events; a foretaste of the Sobell Centre display,

courtesy of "Sword" magazine:

THAI BOXING POSTER   95p

K
O
A

karate

AND ORIENTAL ARTS   No. 119   APR./MAY 1986

Karate

Kung fu

Kendo

Aikido

Ninja

Judo

Jujitsu

Self
Defence

Taekwondo

Martial
Arts

Tai Chi in new form

Kobudo & Nunchaku

Nino Bernardo in California

Donn Draeger in Malaysia

Of course Bruce Lee was not alone in studying weapons systems and their applicability to empty hand combat. Cover of K.O.A. no. 119, 1986 showed the well known and respected hoplologist Donn F. Draeger, with Sifu Cheong Cheng Leong of the Phoenix Eye Fist school. Martial artists from all over the world came to sit at the Sifu's feet to learn. His work with the staff or kun was devastating. *Photo courtesy Francis and Sean Dervan.*

IMPROVISED WEAPONS!
K.O.A. no. 25 for July 1970 had a cartoon by a well known martial
artist, Tony Nelson. It was one of many cartoon contributions which
appeared in the mag. We always kept a lighter note running through
the publication as well as the serious stuff. K.O.A. cost 22.5p - about
33 U.S.A. cents!

The same issue had a piece about Sifu Alan Lee, a Shaolin stylist
with no fewer than eighteen weapons skills to his credit. He had
appeared on the Johnny Carson show where he lay on a bed of
nails, with a 500 lb. slab of stone on his chest, and allowed it to be
smashed with a sledge hammer in the hands of a visiting celebrity.
The article was sent in by Kenneth Cohen. Sifu Lee appeared on
the cover holding the classical Chinese double edged sword.

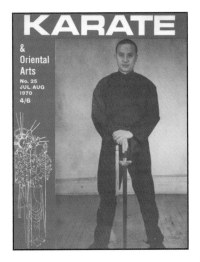

WING CHUN CENTRE LINE & FOIL

One important and controversial technical point about Wing Chun is Centre Line theory. Most students follow the maxim that attacks on an opponent should be made as close as possible to a centre line running down the front of the body. Controversy came with the interpretation of this theory but this does not belong in this section of the book. What is interesting is to hear that in foil fencing, a similar maxim holds:

> In the nature of things engagements tend to be in the middle of the target, down the line of fence, where both fencers... can be attacked on both sides of the blade.
> (Bob Anderson, Olympic Team Coach, in his book
> 'All About Fencing', Stanley Paul, 1970)

Clearly the thinking behind this is the same as the thinking behind Wing Chun. What is so striking is that no one to my knowledge developed this thinking methodcally in connection with western fist fighting. It was left to Bruce Lee, and others of course, to delve into western fencing and draw out the similarities.

When it comes to defence, once again we find favourably comparable methods:

> A fencer attempts to cover himself by lateral movements of his blade, i.e. by *pushing* the opposing blade across, or by changing his engagement from one line to the other.
> (Bob Anderson)

This is definitely similar to Wing Chun. Until this style arrived on the scene, most western students if not all had been used to blocking in a powerful way. This method came from Japanese Karate. More subtle methods of defence were to be found in Okinawan Karate, but in the early days in the West, Okinawan Karate itself was scarce. In Wing Chun the arms are ideally used to guide a punch a little to one side or up or down, so that the defender's body is not disturbed by the move and so that maximum speed can be achieved. Neither time nor energy is used more than they need be. Foil fencing is so, so similar.

COMBINING DEFENCE AND ATTACK

A true innovation for western students, if the above were not innovation enough, was the method of combining a defensive move with an attacking move. In western boxing and in Japanese Karate, a block followed by a counter was the general rule, though there are always exceptions. But to block or rather parry with one arm and hit immediately and smoothly with the same arm was more or less an unknown device.

In foil fencing of course the fencer has no option because he or she is only using one arm anyway. Even so, if you played around at fencing when you were a boy, as I and my friends used to do, pretending to be Errol Flynn, you probably gave your friend's sword quite a whack, when you parried. In his book, Bob Anderson advises the beginner to learn how to "think of the parry and riposte as one move rather than two". This involves lightness, sensitivity and minimum use of lateral space and planes. Pure Wing Chun and later pure Jeet Kune Do.

BODY SHIFTING

The area in which Wing Chun and foil are not similar is in the way the body is permitted to travel through space. Foil is limited to forwards and backwards movement. It is noteworthy that in the early days of western Karate, this was how most of the contests were fought, for several reasons. In Wing Chun, when a student has gone past the early stages of training, he or she learns how to change direction, swivel left or right, and at the same time maintain a position which permits an attack down the centre line. It is only in other more free forms of fencing that this is found.

To keep in a position, or to be able to enter into a position, in which you can find your opponent's centre line is an art in itself, and shows that there is much more to Wing Chun than many students think. This involves expert footwork and some people maintain that you can tell a martial arts expert not by his hands and body work but by his footwork; which makes sense when you remember that the feet do all the major positioning.

This brings up another aspect of Wing Chun and of Bruce Lee's own knowledge of Chinese Martial Arts. There is a style of Kung Fu called Pakua, (Bagua). It is less well known than many others. It is based on constant circling and twisting the torso from left to right at very high speed. Experts in Pakua are hard to touch, let alone hit. One cannot help thinking that Wing Chun centre line application might be very difficult to apply against such experts, because their own centre line is more or less never available. As far as I am concerned this is only speculation as I have never heard of it being tried out. The point being made is that Bruce Lee might never have been in touch with a Pakua expert who might have widened his perspective. Claims have been made that he studied Pakua and other martial arts. I wonder about this. We shall never know. But in connection with fencing, and Pakua application, the use of leaps can be found in both arts as a means of increasing power, speed and overcoming distance. Though it may be used in Wing Chun sometimes it is not found in the three fundamental forms or sets of the art.

Today, many westerners are returning to look at the roots of their own weapons systems, and discovering unexpected knowledge.

The Tao of Jeet Kune Do

Bruce Lee's master work was published in 1975. "The Tao of Jeet Kune Do" or Way of the Intercepting Fist or Stopping Fist, slowly became a steady good seller. This essay is an attempt to look at the book with some degree of impartiality.

In the first place Bruce Lee did not put the final version together himself. By all accounts his notes, writings and jottings were all in a disorganised state. His wife Linda Lee was instrumental in making them available to Rainbow Publications, and a great deal more work had to be done to fashion them into the finished book.

Gil Johnson was a student of Jeet Kune Do and it was he who did the majority of the work of collating the writings. According to Cass Magda, numbers of "the original students of Bruce were involved in helping him sort out the notes, to categorise them and to understand them in the context of what JKD was all about". Sadly, Gil Johnson died in the 1980's.

At the very end of the book, at the foot of the final page, Linda Lee wrote:

> I'd like to express my sincere appreciation to Gil Johnson who has done an excellent job of organizing a mountain of material...

On the varied content of the book, and speaking of JKD in general, Magda says, "Having a central core of something and then exploring and adding other things doesn't make you 'JKD'... Having the Bruce Lee material as your core foundation allows you to see his process, his design, his simplicity and directness. That is the *beginning*. *You then duplicate the process to personalise it with your own experience and study.*" It is essential to grasp this point if you want to understand JKD.

ZEN

The book begins with quotations and ideas from Zen Buddhism. There is no overt mention of Chan Buddhism, sometimes cited as the Chinese precursor of Japanese Zen. The reasons for this may be that at the time Zen was much better known than Taoism or Chan in the West, especially in the United States, and perhaps it was in the Zen form that Lee had encountered the ideas which cast light on his own quest. The opening page has this to say:

> Turn into a doll *made of wood*: it has no ego, it thinks nothing, it is not grasping or sticky.

This reminds one of the story of a fighting cockerel which was being trained for combat, cited by D. T. Suzuki in his book, "Zen and Japanese Culture" (Princeton).

> Chi Hsing Tzu was raising a fighting cock for his lord. Ten days passed and the lord asked, "Is he ready?" Chi answered, "No sir, he is not ready. He is till vain, and flushed with rage." Another ten days passed, and the prince asked about the cock. Chi said, "Not yet, sir, he is alert whenever he sees the shadow of another cock or hears its crowing." Still another ten days passed, and when the inquiry came from the prince, Chi replied, "Not quite yet, sir. His sense of fighting is still smouldering within ready to be awakened." When another ten days elapsed, Chi replied in response to the inquiry: "He is almost ready. Even when he hears another crowing he shows no excitement. He now resembles *one made of wood*. His qualities are integrated. No cocks are his match. They will at once run away from him.

The book continues with the most profound Zen and Taoist sayings and the section ends with a list of the requirements for Buddhism's Eight-Fold Path, widely quoted in books on the subject. The sayings are subjects for reflection, their content sometimes illuminated by moments of insight, and are not Bruce Lee's own in the sense that he was the first to articulate them. His quest brought him into contact with such sayings and he saw that they were related to his quest.

It is difficult, if not impossible, to say how much of Lee's ideas and writings are original, based on realisations and perceptions he had personally, and how much are purely derivative in the sense of he read them first and applied them to his martial arts. The reference already quoted above is an example. To illustrate this further there is the following passage from Dan Inosanto's book, "Art and

Philosophy of Bruce Lee - Jeet Kune Do", Know How Publishing. Inosanto says that Lee went through a period of frustration about an aspect of his training, and Yip Man advised him to take a week off and rest. Whilst travelling on a boat, "suddenly the thought struck him that the very substance which kept him afloat - water - was the embodiment of the ethereal spirit of the martial arts. After all one could strike it and nothing happened. Or one could stab it, and it suffered no dent..." and so forth the train of thought continued.

Anyone who has studied Japanese or Chinese martial arts and done a little reading will be familiar with this idea, the comparison between the yielding power of water (or a willow branch) and the open mind of the martial artist who achieves by not seeking to achieve. The subject, water, is a great symbol in Taoist thought and its virtues are extolled as a major means of beginning to understand a new approach to living as well as fighting.

In the same section of his book, Inosanto distinguishes three levels in training in JKD. The first is when a person knows nothing about martial arts, and when he fights he does so without training, relying on his own reactions, to some extent instinctive. The second level is when he has been taught and trained. The third level is when he sees beyond this techniques and becomes "artless" like water, following where there is a gap, and going around where there is an impenetrable barrier. These levels are, once again, stages described in Taoist and Zen philosophy, and well known to students with a little reading behind them. So to such people, encountering the apparently "new" philosophy of JKD, the question must have come up, "What is all the fuss about?" It is a question which has not to my knowledge been clearly answered by the supporters of JKD.

Since Lee's demise there have been dozens if not hundreds of articles written about JKD, which dance around the basic ideas quoted above. Articles sell magazines, and make newsletters popular, but they do little to explain what makes JKD special as a martial arts philosophy. There is absolutely *nothing* new in it with regard to its *thought*. It may well be that for many of its *students* the philosophy was and is new, *simply because they have never read such things before.* It is a simple fact, not a matter for debate. This does not detract in any way from Bruce Lee's work and efforts. All it does is to put that work and effort into a measure of perspective. Let people who wish merely to promote JKD and those who wish to fantasise about the originality of its thinking cling to their lines, but let the rest of us simply acknowledge what is staring us in the face.

ART

Returning to the TJKD the next section on the Art of the Soul contains statements about the relationship with art and the artist in the widest sense of both words. Once again the section delves into the more subtle aspects and moves on to pages about Jeet Kune Do. These pages show Lee expressing the same thing in different words, as often happens when a person is identified with a subject, it gnaws at him or her, and periodically something is written down in words which seem appropriate.

ORGANIZED DESPAIR

Is the next section heading and here Lee describes examples of the sort of martial arts outlook from which he wishes to distance himself. He says that in martial arts history, for example, "the instinct to follow and imitate seems to be in inherent", and "to find a refreshing, original master teacher is a rarity". Statements like this, generally unqualified, are common in TJKD but this ought not to be levelled at Lee as a criticism. Had he have lived he would most certainly have been persuaded to expand these notes in writing, and might even have employed researchers to find out if it were in fact true that a refreshing, original master teacher is a rarity or not. By definition master teachers of any type are a numerical rarity. And whilst it is true that to follow and imitate is very common, almost out of necessity, there are many examples of students who have gone on to develop variations on, and even developed new arts from, what they first of all followed and imitated.

The interplay in the book is really between the ideal and the practical. Take an animal as an example. A newly born tiger cub will begin to imitate, play and gradually learn to hunt and fight and kill. It is learning the 'classical' methods, the tiger style so to speak. Its weapons, its tools, the teeth and claws and the amazingly muscled body are all at one with the methods it uses. Even if it were feasible, say in the mind of a science fantasy writer, to train the tiger in a different way, could there be another way, and *would it be practical?* Not would it be practical in real life, but practical for the plot of a science fantasy story. As far as a tiger is concerned, the style and the tiger are the best. For purposes of a story you could for instance train the tiger to hunt in packs, surround the prey, close in and thus get lots of meat. There are all kinds of things the fictional tiger might learn to do but essentially its own existing evolved life style and fighting style are the best. That is the practical view. For a martial artist, the practical view is to learn one style and learn it well, and in doing so to train many parts of himself or herself:

reflexes, footwork, conditioning, hitting power,
evasion, blocking, parrying, pacing, and so on...

Then in practical terms he has to adapt his art to the situation, like the tiger. So it is the attitude which is at stake here rather than the techniques of the martial art. In studying different arts, as Lee also advises in the book, you are studying other men's versions of adaptation. Then of course the ideal, to go beyond all this, is a finger pointing at the moon.

TRAINING

The remaining section of the book is about training. Taken with the earlier section it is plain that together they show that Jeet Kune Do is not a homogeneous "system". There are obvious similarities between other famous teaching figures. Their own original motive or drive was peculiar to them. They had the purpose and they found what they found. People who follow them do not have the same purpose or drive, so they have to try to understand what the original teachers were saying. They are talking about what *they* have found, not imparting a formula. In a way we could say that their message is,

"If you were like me, this is what you would say, and this is what you would do. But are you like me?"

The most ingenuous response to this question is to say "yes" merely by dressing up like Bruce Lee. The next may be to repeat what he said and wrote. The next may be to train in what he trained. But the best in a sense would be to try to intuit what he was searching for; what was the core of his search in martial arts.

So as the remaining sections of the TJKD unfold, and we read the references to Wing Chun, western boxing and western fencing, kicking and so forth, we are seeing no more and no less than forays which the martial artist made into these areas, trying them, keeping them, discarding them, to suit his purpose. Treading, even most diligently, in the star's footsteps, does not assure us of understanding.

Some sayings from outside JKD...

He who speaks does not know...
He who knows does not speak.

When I look at a tree and see only
one leaf, I miss the rest...

To do something whether you like
it or not is the sign of a grown up
man or woman...

Nothing is stronger than water...

You scratch my back and I'll
scratch yours...

Give the things of Caesar to Caesar,
give the things of God to God,
and that which is mine give to me...

Undertake great matters as if you
were cooking a small, delicate fish...

Human beings are born peaceful...

Remove your own blindfold before
you remove the speck of dust in your
friend's eye...

A stitch in time saves nine...

To spend your limited life span in
worrying is like weeping into a river
for fear of it drying up...

The shortest distance between two
points is a straight line...

Look before you leap...

If you can meet with triumph and
disaster, and treat those two
imposters just the same...

The longer a fight goes on, the
more chance there is of you being
hurt...

Every stick has two ends...

Let your meat stop your mouth...

Jesus said:
The Kingdom of the Father is as
a man who wishes to kill a giant.
He drew the sword in his house,
he struck through the wall in
order to be assured that his hand
would be confident. Then he
slew the giant...

Real people base their lives on
awareness...

2 + 2 = 4

People who follow the Way
never come to a dead end...

He who rides on a tiger can
never dismount...

Take the wisdom of the East and the science of the West, and then search...

The Weapons
The Rumours
The Realities

**Weapons use quickly entered the Bruce Lee scenario.
This was inevitable since they featured so powerfully in his films. As
usual it was the media that led the way, the public reaction which
followed, and the martial arts fraternity who quietly came up in the
rear.**

Weapons use had already been a regular feature of the martial arts scene long
before Bruce Lee was heard of in the West. It was part of the Japanese and
Okinawan Karate training systems. People knew the story. That when the
Japanese had invaded Okinawa, they had disarmed the population and in
response the largely agricultural Okinawans had used their farming implements
as weapons. A number of styles of weapons use had developed in the Ryukyu
Islands of which Okinawa was the largest, and these had been incorporated into
Karate (Empty Hand) systems. They had travelled to Japan when Karate became
popular there in the 1920's and in succeding decades.

Only when the public imagination was fired by Bruce Lee were these weapons
really perceived as a threat. At first it was the nunchaku in the firing line. The
nunchaku, the chuks, the rice flails, the chukkas, to give them their most common names were held up as a danger to the general population. It was true that
some hooligans began to use them instead of bottles or coshes or whatever they
usually used but the media outcry as usual did not want to get the point. They
wanted to sell newspapers so any garbled story would do.

Rumours spread in the martial arts clubs that the nunchaku were banned.
K.O.A. as usual began to get enquiries about the status of the weapons and
when we investigated ourselves we could find no official reply. It seemed very
much that if a person were stopped by police and nunchaku were found in his
possession it would be up to the officers concerned to decide whether to make
an arrest. The best advice we could give in these circumstances was to say to
people that they should carry nunchaku wrapped up in their martial arts uniform, and this should be kept in their training bag, and that they should only
have them in their possession when travelling to or from a training session.
Then if they were stopped they had a reasonable explanation for having the
weapon in a public place. We had plenty of police officers as customers at the
K.O.A. shop and passed this version of our advice on to them. They seemed to

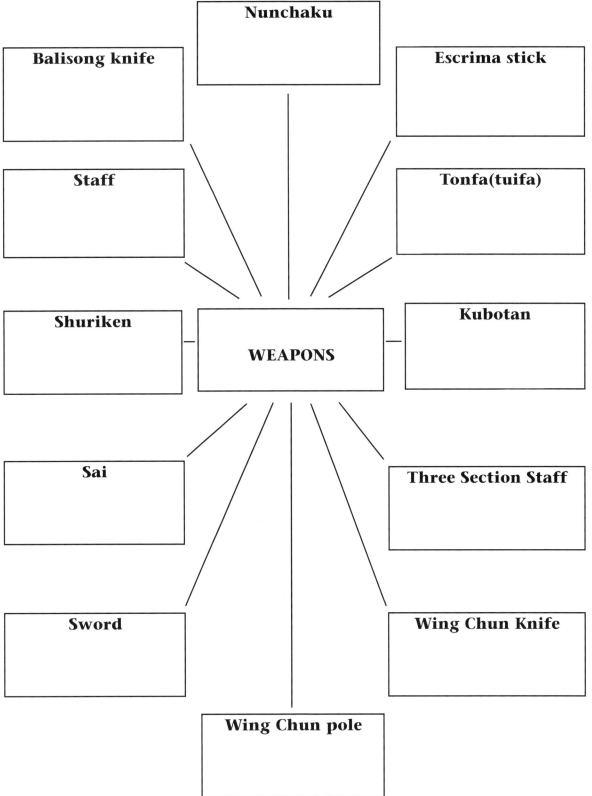

Nunchaku

Balisong knife

Escrima stick

Staff

Tonfa(tuifa)

Shuriken

WEAPONS

Kubotan

Sai

Three Section Staff

Sword

Wing Chun Knife

Wing Chun pole

think this was a fair enough thing to say to people, but they could not be more helpful since they had no official specific instructions themselves. Without the media circus the question might never have come up.

Needless to say, the number of rice flail, nunchaku swinging would-be martial arts weapons students grew. Sequences of Bruce Lee using the chuks were cut from his films by the British Board of Film Censors, and when retailers began to sell videos of the films the regular question became,

"Have you got an uncut version of Bruce using the chuks?"

We didn't... Some pirated versions from Hong Kong kept turning up but we had nothing to do with video piracy.

Rice flails or nunchaku are two pieces of wood joined together by string, leather or chain. Publicity pictures of Bruce Lee showed him wielding what looked like round, tapering black ones joined by chain. The regular Karate weapon was octagonal or hexagonal, usually in plain finish hardwood. These were "out" as far as the fans were concerned. They wanted exact copies of the ones used by their idol. Then a so-called guide to how Bruce Lee used his nunchaku was published and this sold like wildfire. The Karate weapons experts were not impressed. When prospective students asked where they could learn how to use the nunchaku we usually guided them in the direction of some Karate club where they were taught within the disciplines laid down by the style concerned.

Nunchaku which are joined by doubled cord fit very tightly and are difficult to thread up. We spent many a happy hour trying to sort out the fixings of a student's weapon for him in the name of good customer relations.

The number of times we were asked how long the chain was connecting Lee's nunchaku together, I lost count. There was an amusing side to this whole saga. The truth was that there was more harm done by students training badly and hitting themselves on the head or arms or body or legs than there ever was to innocent bystanders. Enterprise quickly solved this situation. Some Einstein of production hit on the notion of making absolutely hollow, plastic chuks, the sort of thing you might find inside a monster Christmas cracker. You could hit yourself on the head with these with every ounce of strength without flinching. These weapons would not have damaged the surface of the proverbial rice pudding, never mind a human skull.

On the same 'striking' note there is the story, true I believe, of a famous Chinese Wing Chun instructor visiting a very tough town in England, Liverpool. How tough the people are can be seen from this tale. He was with a group his students and they got into a fracas with some of the locals in a building with an escalator in it. One of the locals ran away, hotly pursued by the Wing Chun Mr. X. When the local reached the escalator he flew down it, because Mr. X

126

had now 'drawn' his nunchaku. Speedily he let fly at the Liverpuddlian head-now rapidly getting out of kicking range, and expected the victim to fall or at least stop running. The nunchaku hit the man's head, bounced off, and Mr. X watched in astonishment as he continued to run down the escalator without even a break in his stride.

When the aforementioned hollow plastic monster Christmas cracker chuks were dubbed "toy" chuks, enterprise stepped in again with foam chuks. These consisted of a narrow, pencil-like core with foam rubber around the outside to cushion the blow. Then there were the ball bearing chuks, whose action was so fast that the danger to the user increased ten fold. Then there were the wallet size chuks which fitted easily into your inside jacket pocket like a pistol in a shoulder holster. There were other chuk developments later but these are best left in the dark. To even read about them would give delicate readers a nasty shock. Altogether the nunchaku period was one of the many found in the modern world where the originators could never in their wildest dreams have foreseen what would happen to their inventions.

One of the realities of the nunchaku situation in Britain during this lengthy period was the emergence of a Scottish Sensei or teacher called Tom Morris. Not content to wait until some teacher of Okinawan weapons appeared in the country, he took himself abroad and learned intensively the more popular forms: nunchaku, tonfa and bo (staff). People began to learn from him. Another skilled teacher was Steve Arneil, of the Kyokushinkai Karate school. He electrified spectators with a dazzling display of sai (twin daggers). What happened in many instances to these weapons was that they became demonstration props, used like juggling skills. The simple fighting applications became lost in the desire to show off and impress a benighted audience.

You can whirl nunchaku around like a spinning top and catch it in mid-air, throw it between your legs and seize it in front of your abdomen. Meanwhile your opponent has knocked your head off. Basically the nunchaku is a striking weapon, reminiscent of the mediaeval mace and chain, in which the flexible cord or chain gives powerful momentum and stops the impact being transferred back to the user. Skill development should focus on this and the different angles and situations where striking and catching for continued attack are envisaged. Bruce Lee made this perfectly clear!

One writer on censorship called nunchaku "chainsticks". This was a new one on me, but he did make several noteworthy points about them. He said that when Lee used them, the makers had to slow down the film because they moved too fast for people to see them. He also said that a 1989 episode of the "police comedy **Dragnet**" had to be censored because a poster showing nunchaku in use was in the background of one of the shots! Furthermore, some scenes from the Mutant Turtles film had to be censored because they, the miscreants, were actually using the dreaded sociopathic weapons. British fans raised an outcry about the Lee cuts but not the Turtle cuts.

The saga of naming the nunchaku continued with a publication called "Bruce Lee Skill in Two-Piece Rod"; overtones of women's swimming costumes and other delicate matters drifted into mind. This item consisted of film stills of Bruce Lee plus drawings of someone supposed to be the star wielding the two piece rod. At the back it invited fans to "spend ten years to collect the words & rare news of Bruce Lee." Another small promotion in the same publication referred to Bruce Lee's Budo. The last word of course refers to the tradition of Japanese martial ways and would have not gone down well with any Chinese person, let alone Bruce Lee himself.

"Secrets of Kung Fu" magazine added to the vocabulary by calling the nunchaku a Double Staff and so the list grew:

> bnunchaku, chuks, chukkas, rice flails, chain sticks, two piece rod, double staff; the list reminded one of the many names given to hand guns, such as gat, piece, rod, iron, etc.

Sales of book guides to the nunchaku favoured the Bruce Lee publication, simply because of the name, but in fact the Japanese based books were better.

**BUTTERFLY KNIVES
440 STAINLESS BLADES**

525 NINJA	Diecast metal handle, 4" closed	551 SINGAPORE	4¼" closed
527 NINJA	5" closed	552 SINGAPORE	5" closed
526 NINJA	Black metal handle, teflon coated blade, 4" closed	555 SILVER DRAGON	Stainless steel handle, 3¾" closed
528 NINJA	5" closed	556 SILVER DRAGON	4½" closed
530 NINJA	Stainless steel handle with brass lining, 3¾" closed	557 SILVER DRAGON	5¼" closed
531 NINJA	4¼" closed	558 SILVER DRAGON	Stainless steel handle with boot/belt clip, 5" closed
532 NINJA	5" closed	560 BALI HI	Stainless steel handle, 3½" closed
534 CHO	Diecast metal handle, 5" closed	561 BALI HI	4½" closed
535 CHO	Black lacquered handle, teflon coated blade, 5" closed	562 BALI HI	5" closed
550 SINGAPORE	Solid brass handle, 3¾" closed	563 EYE OF THE TIGER	Stainless steel handle with abalone inlay 5" closed

This is a section of an advertisement for Balisong knives. Note the variety, which was in fact much wider, and gradually extended to include knives with wavy guards, so called Ninja type Balisong knives and trench warfare knives. A second stream of knife interest was aroused when martial arts spilled over into survival and Ninjutsu topics fired by films featuring Sho Kosugi, the teachings of the Japanese master Hatsumi and the American Stephen Hayes. Kung Fu, Ninjutsu, Escrima, and martial arts in general became mixed up in some people's minds with the Survival Movement in the U.S.A. and such publications as "Soldier of Fortune".

The most dangerous nunchaku K.O.A. staff ever saw was one made by an American company who supplied the police with weapons. These were made of some very dense substance, probably polycarbonate, and were connected by a single cord of nylon, secured in the usual top hole. The density per cubic centimetre of the nunchaku was frightening. The usual pine wood nunchaku would have been painful on making contact. The oak nunchaku were stronger and more weighty, and there were even nunchaku constructed from rose wood - something of a luxury. But this 'police' style one would have smashed or completely shattered anything it struck, even bricks. It was like launching a ballistic missile.

A more serious note still was struck when Balisong knives made their appearance. These weapons were originally from the Philippines and were associated in the martial arts world with Escrima and the martial arts of the Filipinos. It also bore the name of "butterfly knife" because the handle consisted of two hinged covers for the blade, and could be flicked open and locked into place by a small hinged catch. Somewhat in the "tradition" of the nunchaku, more attention was paid by western fans of the Balisong to the intricate patterns in the air which could be made than the practical use which occupied the originals users. The Balisong is associated with the Arnis Lanada style of Filipino martial arts. In the late 1970's and the 1980's a famous teacher and practitioner was Porfirio S. Lanada, who brought the system to life. Knives have always had a fascination for martial artists, mainly because they are so difficult to deal with in the hands of a trained man or woman. The Balisong is no exception. The methods shown of doing this, in 95% of martial arts guides to self defence are pure rubbish, and a danger to people who read them and believe them. Just remember the last time you cut yourself, in the kitchen or working with a knife on some job around the house. You probably made a little slip, without much force, and you were cut. Then imagine what that cut could be like if someone had attacked you and used the knife with force and accuracy. It doesn't bear thinking about.

People who can use knives have very simply thought about the best way, in the same way as you might think of the best way to build a small wooden shed. The chief difference between you is not that you could not think the same things and work out how to use a knife; the difference is that you don't think about things like that. It is always a shock when someone looks at knife fighting; the cold blooded simplicity...

The Filipino Balisong masters worked out, some say with the influence of Mexican knife fighting, intricate patterns of use. When seen they look aesthetically pleasing, but the purpose is to strike the vital points of the body as quickly as possible and with the minimum effort and minimum waste of movement. It is the type of thing that the S.A.S., Green Berets and other specialised units are taught. When the Balisongs appeared in the European martial arts scene, there was a flurry of interest, but it died down. At the same time there was a note of concern in official places and a sigh of relief must have been heard in many quarters when there was no sign of knife or blade using in the later Bruce Lee films. The Filipino influence stayed at the level of sticks in the films. Another weapon, briefly popular during the martial arts boom was the three-section-staff. This looked like a monster nunchaku, with three sticks joined together instead of two. It was not practical to carry such a weapon in the pocket and even a training bag was too small. The three-section-staff remains principally a film weapon and one used by Wushu (traditional) Chinese martial artists for competition and display.

A modern adaptation of an old weapon is the Kubotan, brainchild of Tak Kubota. In Japan the use of sticks of all sizes in defence and attack is well known. The shorter ones, with varying types of grip, were especially used to strike vital points, apply pressure and help in attacking joints. Kubota took this simple notion and produced a pencil-long cylinder with a key ring at one end and gave it his own name, adding an 'n'. The name 'Kubotan' was registered as a trademark, and so other manufacturers could not legally use it. An alternative title was needed and one company came up with the expression 'Persuader'. In England the weapon was introduced to the police force and met with a certain amount of approval. It's chief positive feature was the fact that in the hands of a trained person it could be used to jab or press powerfully at a vulnerable spot. People whose hands were not so strong, large or tough could benefit from such a feature.

Wing Chun has large broad "daggers" in its repertory but these too have never caught on anything like the nunchaku. The art also has a very long pole in its arsenal, up to ten feet long. Just to hold it out horizontally straight requires strength. But finally it is the old rice flail, nunchaku, chained sticks, double rods for which Bruce Lee is remembered in the weapons field. Today, nunchaku popularity has shrunk to a fraction of what it was among fans. It is chiefly in the ranks of Karate students that enthusiasts are found. The days of the nunchaku "terror" are long since gone.

Overlapping the nunchaku craze was the "death star" craze, sparked off by the Ninja craze but first brought to the attention of westerners in "You Only Live Twice", at least a decade earlier. Best authentic book on the subject is "Shurikendo" by Shirakami Ikku-ken.

Bruce Lee came from a long line of people who were interested in physical development...

The Chinese, Persians, Egyptians, Greeks and Romans all had methods of developing the physiques of their athletes and armies. In the early part of this century, the Chinese government tried to popularise martial arts and exercise to improve the health of the nation. The large number of martial arts and exercise systems, the knowledge of herbs and acupuncture, and the now very popular arts of chi kung (qigong) in China testify to the perennial interest of the Chinese people in the human body, in the widest sense.

When I was a boy, a friend gave me a copy of a book by the Bavarian strong man, Maxick. He was born in 1882 and in 1909 he came to London, England and took the world of body building and muscle control by storm. Interestingly, in common with many famous martial arts masters and health experts, he himself had been a very weak and sickly child. Determined to overcome this he studied as a boy how to isolate muscle contraction, taking muscles to the limit. He watched other people going about their jobs and noticed how each trade or profession had its own physical imbalance. By training in the ways he discovered and invented he developed very good concentration and attention to his body. At the age of 79 and weighing only 110 lbs. he defeated a man 35 years younger and 108 lbs. heavier in an arm wrestling contest. Nearly twice his weight.

I was never interested in body building but being able to isolate muscles by relaxing the muscles not needed to perform a movement was what attracted me. I studied Maxick's little book and tried his methods to the best of my ability. It worked. Later this helped me in martial arts training and in Tai Chi studies.

This was clearly something which appealed also to Bruce Lee, and stories are told of his remarkable muscle control ability. This does depend a great deal on concentration or the ability to keep attention on the muscles and body balance. The way he could maintain his balance, though having one leg shorter than the other, by all accounts, and at the same time deliver a very effective blow with hand or leg, is a testimony to his skill in this direction.

What is also very important in developing such ability is the capacity to relax the muscles which are not used in the strike. Lee had this too, otherwise he could not possibly have moved at the speed he displayed. If you look at any animal, wild or domestic, you will notice this relaxation. In particular the cat family are very clear examples. The power of the tiger, and its impressive movements come as much from its inherent relaxation as its contraction. It is the Yin-Yang principle in living action.

The strange and much imitated noises which

Lee made in his fight scenes also played a practical role in developing his speed. Many animals growl or make sounds as they prepare to fight. In my view, it is not just to frighten the enemy, stir up the blood and so forth, but also to communicate through sound, through vibration to the rest of the body and harmonise its activity, relaxation and contraction.

Bruce Lee was a keen dancer, and winner of Cha-Cha competitions as we know, and everyone is aware of the fact that good dancing requires relaxation, so that the body can express the rhythm well. Students of Dan Inosanto and others are encouraged to train to music, drum beats, and so forth to bring rhythm and therefore relaxation into their martial arts.

What seems to have been a troublesome aspect of Lee's training methods, however, is not the subject of relaxing and contracting but of having sufficient energy to do what he wanted to do, martial arts wise. We gather that he wanted to have *instant access* to energy supplies. This is a difficult question, and a dangerous one, because it involves the vital processes of the body, and not simply muscle control. It is known about world wide through the misuse of anabolic steroids and other drugs by even Olympic athletes. What they want and what Bruce Lee seemed to want is instant explosive energy: to sprint, swim, jump, leap, punch and kick as required, at the touch of a button.

In this situation, it is not a matter of a struggle for skill and a matching of skill but a matching of energy supply, a struggle for a superior energy supply. In several films and books, Bruce Lee's preoccupation with obtaining the energy-result is underlined, and the degree to which he drove himself is some-times cited as a contributing factor to his death. In the days of the boom the story went around, as if it were a piece of science fiction, that the star had a special training apparatus consisting of wires attached to his body leading to a monitor where he could gauge the activity of each muscle. Though it was unusual for an individual to have such a thing, it was not unusual in the labs. of students of physiology. Bruce Lee, with characteristic determination, had apparently got one of his own!

According to his family and friends, there were few, if any, systems of muscle training that the star had not tried. Also, he was very fond of food and drink supplements, healthy diet and many modern systems of nutrition. There is little mention of traditional Chinese herbs, diet or training methods. One big exception was of course the Wing Chun dummy and Chi Sao training. These were two of the foundations of his martial arts skills. Apart from the sequence drills learned from the dummy, the act of repeatedly coming into contact with a hard wooden surface conditions the forearms to take blows and be resilient to them.

Isometrics, using weights, devising resistance apparatus, specialised food and drink, all formed part of Bruce Lee's programmes, but they are not peculiar to him. Thousands of others used the same things, more or less. What singled Lee out was the combinations which he arrived at and his own amazing powers of concentration. It is always the same. It is not the style which counts, it is the man or woman who is using it. As well it is very much a question of relaxation. As the famous Tai Chi master Yang Cheng-fu used to say: Relax, just relax. And when asked for more advice he would say: Relax, just relax.

The idea that stretching should play a big part in martial arts training led to a boom in the publication of books on the subject. Apparatus for stretching the legs accompanied this boom and ranged from simple pulleys fixed to the ceiling to special machines costing hundreds of pounds. Around the world, studies appeared proving that this or that method should be used, and magazine articles fed the students' hunger for more and more information.

Bruce Lee's own interest in stretching and his attitudes to its importance gave an additional push to the subject. As is sometimes the case when anything becomes popular, the work of serious researchers in the field is not always top of the promotion list. Serious work of this type had been done by teachers of ballet and of dance in general. It followed in the scientific steps of the study of somatotyping. This is the grouping of three basic physical types of the population in general, without reference to athletics, dancing or martial arts. Each type has certain characteristics with accompanying strengths and weaknesses with regard to exercise.

So to take a simple example, a short legged, squarely built, heavy muscular man who might excel at weight lifting is not a suitable type for marathon running. A slim, taller and skinnier man is not a suitable type for weight lifting but is more at home in marathon running. The first man is also a candidate for much more stretching exercises than the second man, who is already likely to be loose and 'stretched'. The first man is physically 'tighter' and needs stretching more. This type of analysis of course needs more time, more knowledge and more attention devoted to it, and martial arts students on the whole were not prepared to find out about it, or more likely, did not know about it.

Similar things can be said about weight training, the number of repetitions to be done, the size of weights and so forth. Since the Rome Olympics of 1960 the scientific approach to sport has been emphasised and many measurements of, and comparisons between, athletes have been made. One very simple and striking point concerns the place at which a muscle is inserted.

The biceps muscles are used for bending the arm, and so for lifting any weight, pulling any opponent and so on. The tendons at the bottom of the biceps, or at the point furthest a way from the shoulder, insert into, or are fixed into, the top part of the forearm, nearest the elbow. The distance from the elbow at which this insertion point is made is not the same in everyone, which is not surprising. But what follows from this, in terms of simple mechanics, is that the further the insertion point is from the elbow, the more weight a given quantity of muscular exertion can produce.

So if you have two men, with an insertion point difference of say one inch, arm lengths being more or less equal, one man can lift X pounds of weight using 5 units of force, but the other man can lift X plus pounds using the same number of units. Limb length was mentioned, and the part this plays in performance is even more obvious. Scientific measurement and comparison of many aspects of the builds of athletes accumulated. Unfortunately, this knowledge did not filter through into the martial arts world, apart from a few isolated cases and so its benefits were ignored.

What particularly was upsetting for me was the sight of proud fathers coming into the K.O.A. shop wanting their sons to become a martial arts experts at a very young age, and asking my advice as if I were an authority on child athletic development. My own thoughts were that to begin putting a youngster, under ten years old, through a strict training regime, using apparatus and pushing him hard, was wrong. It seemed far better for him to play games and let his body grow and mature of its own accord.

Yet there were the physique and martial skills of Bruce Lee staring everyone in the face, and the urge to be like the star was very strong.

May 1983, in KOA no. 102 we marked the tenth anniversary of Bruce Lee's death.

Steve Lee Swift, then a pupil of Sifu Simon Lau, and formerly an American Karate Champion, based in Chicago, featured in a lead article on Wing Chun.

Swift had been trained by Kickboxing World Champion Bill Wallace.

Lau was engaged in filming for Gold Crest Productions, "Body Machine", and spoke on Capital Radio about Bruce Lee.

PART THREE
MEDIA REACTIONS

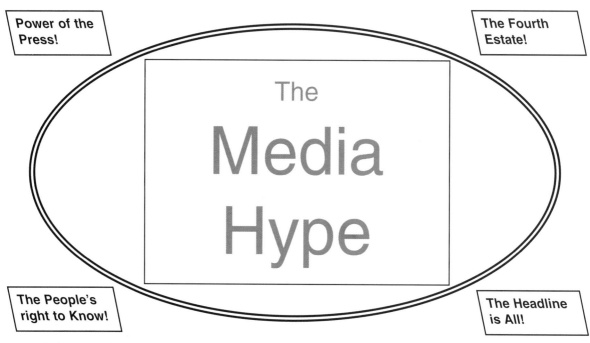

Power of the Press!

The Fourth Estate!

The People's right to Know!

The Headline is All!

It is a well known fact that journalists have to make a living. We say in general that we do not like them, as a species, but we buy what they write and so what's the problem? This reminds me of the best martial arts film ever made, "The Seven Samurai", directed by Kurosawa. In one scene the samurai have discovered that one of their number was originally a farmer and even so accept him though he is not from a samurai family. They then discover that the farmers who have hired them for protection against brigands have deceived them.

The farmer-samurai turns on the real samurai and in a mixture of rage and pain explodes with the accusation that the samurai made the farmers what they are: deceitful, greedy and untrustworthy. The samurai, as a class, steal from the farmers, rape their women folk, and treat them like slaves. What do the samurai expect in return? The hired samurai absorb this piece of direct philosophy with a mixture of martial calm and judicial reflection.

Probably we, the readers of newspapers, have made journalists what they are. They certainly lived up to expectations as far as the Bruce Lee phenomenon was concerned.   If we want page three girls, displaying their breasts, we get them. If we want headlines bordering on lies, we get them. And if we want news with a political slant, we get it. If we want generalisations covering up a lack of solid information we get that too.

karate
AND ORIENTAL ARTS   75p   AUG./SEPT. 1984   No. 109

TIGERS OF MUAY THAI!

During this heady period, even some seasoned reporters lost their heads. I was in the K.O.A. shop one day, alone, without any witnesses. A very well known reporter, whose name was bandied about in the press and on the B.B.C. whizzed into the shop and introduced himself.

I did not come to attention and salute, as his manner clearly indicated that I should, but waited. His paper was one of the oldest and most respected in Brtain at the time. He said that he had seen K.O.A. magazine and noticed a really good action photograph inside it and wanted to have it published in his paper. I said that I was not sure about this. Why was it to be used, I asked, and similar questions. He was offended that I did not immediately agree., and said, "If you don't agree, there are ways and means you know". What happened following this virtual threat is between him and me.

This was one of the covers of K.O.A. in 1984 supplied by Martyn K. Evans for our lead story Master Sken Kaepadung, Muay Thai.

It differed very little from the covers of other magazines the world over.

In Germany, the publication "Karate Magazin" for December 1975 had a full page cover of David Carradine in the television series "Kung Fu", with a brief article on the star inside. The rest of the magazine was devoted to Karate and Professional Karate exclusively. David Carradine and Kung Fu were merely selling points.

Bruce Lee was similarly used both to sell magazines and products, courses and promote some bogus teachers. This became par for the course! The public were all at sea.

The public wanted to know about Bruce Lee, and also Kung fu. The press, the journalists, wanted to know so that they could give the public what they wanted. The problem was, who was Bruce Lee and what was Kung fu? I got a call from a journalist who worked for a paper called "Reveille", now defunct. He plainly knew nothing about anything that he wanted to know about. He wanted me to tell him what he should ask me. He would have written an article if I had given him one word. He would have taken that word, like a postage stamp, and moulded it and stretched it, and bent it, and coloured it and bleached it until he had a sheet of paper as big as the page of a tabloid. Oh, the magic of the man!

I made a bargain with him. I would tell him something if he quoted the name of our magazine, K.O.A., in his article, and if he guaranteed that it would be published and not edited out of his article. I did this with every journalist who got in touch. In that way we spread the demand for our own publication. It was the best we could do, because sooner or later a journalist will find out something; he has to in order to survive.

At first it was Kung fu on the agenda. There was the usual quota of corny jokes that Kung fu was the name of a chain of Chinese Takeaways. That Kung fu students wore black pyjamas. That Kung fu turned a person into a killer, and like Karate-ka their hands should be licensed as weapons. Some enterprising publisher produced a book on Kung fu with all the line drawings showing people doing Karate. It probably sold very well; how were the public to know?

In our shop, which backed up the magazine, we had for some years sold only good, recognised books on solid, traditional styles of martial arts, together with others which explained eastern philosophies, written by experts in the field. As the media hype of martial arts continued, real unadulterated unhelpful rubbish began to be published; stuff which misled the public and gave them wrong ideas about martial arts. Journalists and ghost writers were clearly having a field day.

The distressing thing for traditional martial artists, who had in some cases devoted most of their lives to a style or group of styles, was that the public were buying these publications like people dying of thirst in the desert buying water. People came into our shop, and nine out of ten of them were not interested in books by Nishiyama, or Robert Smith or Donn F. Draeger. They wanted the deadly art of Kung fu written by Joe Bloggs, the well known market gardener from Epping Forest! Or how to kill all your enemies in one blow by Wong Wong Wong, the Chinese waiter from Gerrard Street. If a person had a Chinese face, he was obviously a Kung fu master. If he had blue eyes and fair hair he was obviously a nobody.

At the same time, Kung fu experts began to appear from nowhere. Once Fulham or Peckham or Birmingham or Glasgow or Torquay had been Kung fu free zones; now there was a Kung fu master on every street corner, his open hand ready, not to fight but to take your money. People who had been trained in Aikido or Karate would also suddenly become Kung fu experts. One of the martial arts jokes about this was that when asked, such a person would say he had learned his art from a Chinese sailor who only came to Britain infrequently, so there was no chance of getting in touch with him to verify the claim.

"Deadly Hands" and "Death Blows" and "Secret Techniques" became the order of the day. Correspondence courses from some post office box number or other sprouted. "Learn in the privacy of your own home"(where you will learn nothing useful) came the comforting message, which failed to add, like Red Riding Hood's wolf, "all the better to fleece you with my dear".

In the end, in order to survive, the K.O.A. shop, with cheeks red with shame, had also to climb on the bandwagon. We ended up selling rubbish to the undiscerning and the best to the discerning. We explained this to our old customers and they nodded in understanding sympathy. It was no use telling the public what was in their best interests. They wanted the hype and they bought it.

Then Bruce Lee and to a much lesser extent David Carradine of the Kung fu television series fame made their entrances. Carradine's image immediately appeared as a Kung fu master. It slowly became clear to the staff of K.O.A. that many people really believed that the actor, David Carradine, could himself, in real life, actually do what the episodes shown each week to a very large viewing audience portrayed him as doing. To be sure, if questioned, people would have denied it, in cold blood, but secretly in a part of themselves they thought that he could.

"Does David Carradine do Kung fu, and what style?" became a standard question for us to answer. Readers may know that the

most famous place in the public mind for studying Kung fu was the
Shaolin Temple, which translated means Small Forest Temple.
Fans were ready and able, if the Chinese government of the time had
permitted them, to hike themselves off to the temple and seek out
David Carradine's master, who of course was an actor. No matter that
the temple as shown on television was nothing more than a studio lot.
Fans were going to find it, or something like it, somewhere in China.
They would ask where it was when they got there! After all, China
was a place where people more or less thought about Kung fu all day
long. Work? Forget it.

Meantime, publishers and journalists were still hot on the trail.
Making contact after contact, the real McCoy on Bruce Lee and Kung
fu was coming out. One writer, plumbing the depths of Kung fu wisdom, and writing about Lee's philosophy came out with the words,
"Thus spoke Hojo Tokiyori, a famous thirteenth century general, who
was instrumental in the speed of Zen Buddhism..." He probably
meant the "spread" of Zen Buddhism, not amphetamines, but even if
the error were one of proof reading it still unhappily fitted the journal-
istic bill of the time. Another publication advertised itself as containg
"Scores of photos of The Master in action". It was literally true, it had
41 photos of Bruce Lee in action.

In 1974 a veritable masterpiece appeared called "Bruce Lee, My
Martial Arts Training Guide 'Jeet Kune-Do'". This seventy page wonder promised much but gave little.

"The main characteristic of this style (JKD) is the absence of the usual
classical passive blocking." Was one of the writer's pearls of knowledge. "Blocking is the least efficient," he went on. "Jeet Kune Do is
offensive, it's alive and it's free." JKD might have been free but the
publication wasn't! Precisely what these sentences mean is a mystery
to this day. If he meant that blocking is the least efficient way of
attacking, then he is probably right.

What the writer of this epic did was to take a few ideas without giving
them any real perspective, mix in some photos of Lee in action, mainly shots from his films, mix in some Wing Chun, take some photos
from one of Lee's earliest books and give the result the above title.
But as we have already agreed, journalists have to make a living. How
they got away with the title is a mystery. Some trading standards offi-
cer might have had a field day!

Another hype, followed by the media, was the type which provided members of parliament with ammunition to get their names into the newpapers. Without mentioning any names the form was as follows. Every now and then a question would be asked about the dangers of the widespread training in martial arts which was infecting the country. Men with little or no knowledge of what they were "very concerned" about were very concerned, and would voice their fears about the threat to the nation, and the effects on the Cold War, which might result from people learning Karate and Kung fu. To be fair, such concerns made no distinction between the two.

Visions of wild gangs of Karate students, still in their Karate-gi and bare footed rushing through quiet villages and punching the lights out of innocent old ladies disturbed the sleep of the nation. No one was safe from the Karate chop or the deadly Kung fu blow. Anyone might fall victim. Irish navvies and building site hod carriers quaked in their boots, and the S.A.S. were on red alert in case martial artists stormed the Russian embassy!

As in all emergencies, a Commission was proposed to Control the spread of infection. The British Karate Control Commission came into being. The attitude of the authorities was nothing if not fair. When Kung fu joined the fray it was mooted that Kung fu and Karate could all come under the same umbrella. It was some time before martial artists could make it clear that the two classes of art were different. There would have been much more likelihood of a riot if the leading figures in Karate and Kung fu had been on the same committee than there ever would have been of a riot from martial arts students.

This problem was a strange one, considering that separate bodies are readily set up for the most obscure sports, yet for two distinct arts, one from Japan and one from China, with followers at one time going into tens of thousands, the authorities were unable to see this distinction, or, if they were able, were unwilling to act on it. Occasionally the thought would occur to me that the reason lay in the fact that the leading figures in all these arts were for many years foreigners - Japanese Sensei and Chinese Sifu. Was there an element of racial/political prejudice? It was reported that English Kendo and Iaido (Japanese swordsmanship) practitioners found it hard to get a hall in which to practice because of local prejudice against things Japanese, harking back to the Second World War. So maybe something of the same influenced the authorities' thinking in the early days. Meantime, some serious paperback publishing was gathering momentum. In 1973, Universal Award House Inc.

in the United States published "Enter the Dragon - Kung fu killers on the loose - Now an action-packed film starring Bruce Lee", written by Mike Roote, from the original screenplay by MIchael Allin. In 1974 Tandem books published it in England. It was the story of the film, in novel form. Fans could savour the words whilst re-living the images. In 1975 Star Books, based on the Isle of Man, produced "The Life and Tragic Death of Bruce Lee". The words "by his wife Linda" adorned the title page. The "exclusive" illustrations promised on the cover were few. The book made a very interesting read and sold very well. It had been published in the U.S.A. under the title "Bruce Lee - the man only I knew" by Warner. Indeed if anyone deserved to be a beneficiary of Lee's legacy it was of course his own wife, and children. When I spoke to an American lawyer in 1998 about Bruce Lee's work and life he remarked that, "There's been a lot of skull duggery...," and left it at that.

In Hong Kong, where regard for an individual's rights in showbiz have always been a grey area, copying of pictures of Bruce Lee was an epidemic. With or without permission, images of the star flooded the island and travelled in tens of thousands to worldwide destinations. One of the more enjoyable novelties exported were known in Britain as the Bruce Lee Flick Books. These were action sequences from his films on consecutive pages, and when you flicked the pages through quickly you could watch Bruce Lee in action, like a movie. Translations on these items were quaint and amusing, the covers describing the contents as, "Lively, Active, Frisky" and "Using papers to produce a sense of movement". Volume 2 of this flick book series showed the star in action with the censored nunchaku so how could anyone resist? "You only have to pay a small sum of money," went the legend, "and you can enjoy Bruce Lee in Motion Pictures at any time without a film projector." Wowee!

Shoulder to shoulder with people who produced these items were the producers of a series of magazine format books which were in constant demand:

Bruce Lee's Nunchaku in Action
Bruce Lee: His Privacy & Anecdotes
Studies on Jeet Kune Do
Bruce Lee: the Secret of Jeet Kune Do & Kung fu
Bruce Lee: His Unknowns in Martial Arts Learning
Bruce Lee: Revenges...
Bruce Lee in "The Game of Death"
Bruce Lee: The Fighting Spirit
Bruce Lee Combats
Reminiscence of Bruce Lee
Bruce Lee: The Immortal Dragon
Bruce Lee's Game of Death Extract Edition

The tone of much of the writing about Bruce Lee was of the "we love Bruce" variety, as if Bruce Lee were personally known to everyone and we all missed him terribly and what a great guy he was (as long as the dollars rolled in).

Meantime back on the Isle of Man, Star Books produced another paperback called "Bruce Lee Lives?", in 1975 by someone called Max Caulfield. This was a fictional dramatic reconstruction of an investigation into whether the star were still alive or not. It began with a number of facts about Bruce Lee, and then diverted into a James Bond like yarn, which ended inconclusively. One memorable paragraph is where the writer refers to, "the noted boxer, wrestler and martial arts expert John Gilbey"; noted of course because John Gilbey is the pen name of... ? No prizes for a correct guess. I guess that the real writer has had a few laughs and rueful smiles over the references in print to him under his soubriquet.

During the same period, Jafaha Publications in Manila, Philippines, produced its "maiden" edition of Martial Arts Magazine, hailing Dan Inosanto as "the only Pilipino student of Bruce Lee", in its headline, thus showing that their proof readers and spelling team needed a good talking to. A photo of Dan holding two kris-like blades was on the cover, with Bruce Lee film shots in the background. It also contained a personal letter from Dan in which he expressed his dismay that the "Filipino Hands Arts are dying out in the Philippines". He said that the (empty) hand arts are traditionally only taught to senior students, and that the hand arts are second only to Jeet Kune Do. The letter had a touching intimacy about it. Illustrations in the magazine looked as though they had been borrowed from other publications and the quality was not good.

On a similar note to that expressed by Inosanto, a later issue of the magazine, vol. 2 no.2, had a piece by Rene J. Navarro on Gilas Arnis, who wrote"

> But we tend to downgrade our own culture... When it is a Chinese martial artist who speaks, or a Japanese or Okinawan, we listen. We recognise the value of our own art only when we have seen it arrive in America.

How true! But be that as it may, the magazine continued to give eminence to Bruce Lee in various forms, and the flood of kung fu and karate figures and themes which followed in his wake. The truth was that the hype machines in Hong Kong and Tokyo and the U.S.A. were far more powerful than those of the Philippines, and Kali, Escrima and Arnis came very low on the list of their priorities. It was not the fact that Arnis had arrived in America that gave it any press space, but the fact that Dan Inosanto was a friend and pupil of Bruce Lee. Otherwise, these arts might still be completely unknown. Noteworthy for karate students in issue Vol. 1 no. 2 of the Filipino magazine were a series of almost invisible photographs of the legendary "Cat" Yamaguchi of Goju fame shown doing pre-arranged sparring with a pupil, and wearing a hakama, or split skirt. The same issue gave a brief history of the rise of kung fu in Manila's Chinatown.

This was one of the plus signs beside the Bruce Lee media hype. It brought to the surface a great deal of knowledge which might otherwise have simply disappeared from lack of interest. We can thank the moguls of hype for this at least.

An enormous tome would be needed to chart the world wide hype campaign. What you are reading here gives you a taste of it.

On the next page you see the advertisement for our books which appeared in a very large, newspaper format publication produced by New English Library, London in 1974. It was titled very simply: 'Bruce Lee' and had a picture of the star holding his nunchaku horizontally before him. This was a real stroke of luck for K.O.A. because the publishers needed to mention some titles which readers could buy, and the advertisement was free. We were very grateful to NEL for that.

We were also very grateful to whoever edited and proof read the magazine because there was an 'error in our favour', to quote the famous lines from Monopoly. In addition to the advertisement there was a written description of our book on Wing Chun. It read:

> *This, the first book on Wing Chun Kung Fu ever published outside China, is a practical guide and introduction to the art. A series of photographs and instructions show the Siu Lim Tao Kato...*

The free publicity and the mention of Wing Chun was very, very good for us. But the misprint of "Kato" was excellent, because Kato was the name Bruce Lee had had in his television appearance in the "Green Hornet", in the United States. Fans thought that the photographs of Siu Lim Tao which were of the co-author Greco Wong ,were photos of Kato, i.e. Bruce Lee in his role of Kato. Fortunately when we sold the book we were never accused of misrepresentation and of course it was not our fault.

What had happened was that in trying to explain to NEL editors what the book was about we had said that Siu Lim Tao was a Kung Fu Set or Form, like a Kata in Karate. Kata was a word that westerners were more familiar with at this time. The unfortunate editor had thought we meant Kato.

KUNG FU & KARATE

BOOKS - MAGAZINES - SUITS

"Praying Mantis Kung Fu"
£2.35

"Wing Chun Kung Fu"
£2.35

"Inside Kung Fu"
Magazine 50p

"Karate & Oriental Arts"
Magazine 35p

SEND S.A.E. FOR LISTS

PAUL H. CROMPTON LTD.
638 Fulham Road, London S.W.6.

The
advertisement
which
appeared free
of charge
in the NEL
publication in
1974.

Please note
that the prices
and the
address
have changed.

Pilgrims to
638
Fulham Road
will find there
are no
relics left
there
and the
new
proprietor will
definitely not
be happy
to see you.

True journalists to the end, NEL also gave an excellent description of the special punching techniques of what they thought was Chinese Kung Fu. Regardless of what they had written in other parts of the publication, and without consulting anyone who knew what he was talking about, someone penned the technique of basic Japanese Karate punching!!! Martial artists smiled their superior smile. Journalists have deadlines to meet.

Thanks NEL...

In the midst of all the media hype, another item surfaced and was the subject of endless controversy and speculation. This was the mail order course promoted by "Honourable Master Leong Fu...Retired undefeated Chinese Kung Fu Champion of the World, the Greatest Living Authority of the Chinese Art of Self Defence, Conqueror of more than 100 of the World's Best Professional Kung Fu Exponents of Various Styles, Schools, Sects, Caves and Monasteries..." and so on. Caves...? I swapped a copy of the course with a customer, for the archives...

The system was called Chinese Kung-Fu (Atado) Karato and consisted of at least twelve separate bundles of illustrations of various self defence, judo, jujutsu and other fighting moves. It first appeared in 1958(?), copyright Leong Fu, and the Bruce Lee boom provided it with fertile soil for rapid growth. I seem to remember that at the height of the fever it was produced in one volume as a very expensive hard cover book. The course was widely advertised and appealed to the least critical of martial arts fans, with its lurid cover drawings and the implications of unparalleled power. On the back of the course was a photograph of man dressed as a wrestler, thick set and strong looking. Leong Fu?

It infuriated many KOA readers and customers for a variety of reasons and more than one hot discussion was heard in the KOA shop, which now bore the nickname of Crompton's Aladdin's cave, about the authenticity of the writer, the name of his course, the contents of the course. The biggest thorn in the flesh was that no one had ever seen Leong Fu; no one could find out where he was; others said that he was really Mr. So-and-So, etc., etc. In any case, the sale of the course was fuelled by the mystery.

In Hong Kong, the publication race had another competitor in the shape of a magazine called "Secrets of Kung Fu", published in English, which featured many authentic teachers, techniques of Kung Fu, shots from films, questions and answers, ancient Chinese legends and lore, and the usual wealth of strange translations into English which were a hallmark of the genre. As far as I am concerned these were touchingly humorous. For instance a letter published in Vol. 1 no. 5 to the editor Professor C. Y. Wong began:

> I greatly respect, Late - Bruce Lee for operation in Double Staff, as my neighbour, a youth who taught me Double Staff operation, now I can handle fluent... I would like to have my further study, in necessity to seek for Double Staff...

An article on Claw techniques of Kung Fu, like the above extract, had you hanging on to your seat, waiting for sentences to unfold; the verbal excitement for me was tangible. I in no way looked down on these efforts at English; they were in a sense more interesting than the articles themselves:

> Both Human digitals and claws are no match for those of hawks and tigers, nor that of rats and insects as a weapon. The sight of a hawk preying on a crane or a mantis victimising an insect, will make a human admit inferiority.

The same issue of "Secrets" made historical and social claims which might not be favoured by academics:

> Kung Fu is a defensive medium to procure peace while Acupuncture guarantees good health and prosperous propagation. Thus, China ranks highest in population and this is perhaps a credit of the above mentioned.

In other articles the English was just like in England and the ideas sound. The contents included:

> Developing Iron Palm
> How the ancient Chinese beseiged a city
> Understanding Chinese Kung Fu
> Photo of Bruce Lee with Shek Kin and others
> Walking on clay pots for balance and agility
> Self Defence
> Training schedules for digital offensives
> The miraculous lash of Sifu Lau Chi Ming
> Instructions for Claw Offensive Drills

and more. All in all, just what martial arts fans were looking for. The quaint language perhaps even gave the magazine a flavour of greater authenticity.

Of course, Bruce Lee was never far away from the editor's thoughts, and the contentious subject of Wing Chun occasionally haunted its pages. This magazine was not really a part of the hype brigade and shed much light on the whole of the Kung Fu scene in Hong Kong and later in the West. The most respected publication in Hong Kong, published only in Chinese, was the 92 page 'New Martial Hero", in which all manner of combat arts, not just Kung Fu, was presented, and the more serious questions of the day thrashed out by editor and readers. Once again, features on Bruce Lee fired the interest of all. Hong Kong loved Lee; in a way...

In 1974, Sphere books produced a tome called 'Beginners Guide to Kung Fu'. On the cover was the Japanese Rising Sun symbol, similar in appearance to the emblem of the Shotokan Karate schools of the time. An eastern gentleman was punching oi-zuki (karate lunge punch) at the reader on the cover. Authors Felix Dennis and Paul Simmons warned readers that 'Kung Fu is not a game', and that 'the most secret of the murderous Chinese Martial Arts is, essentially, a defensive technique - the kind that cripples an opponent'. With these strangely contradictory words, these two expert(?) authors introduced readers to a smattering of kung fu history, a rapid three page course in abdominal breathing, and we were off into, no, not Kung Fu, but, you've guessed it, Karate. Front kicks, side kicks, roundhouse kicks, back kicks, and so on.

A few Jujutsu techniques were thrown in for good measure, and to finish, a woman in very high heels was showing what she could do to a plastic man standing still in front of her. He must have been plastic because otherwise the defensive 'kung fu' methods she was using would not have worked. Either that or he had just drunk a whole bottle of whiskey!

In one memorable scene she is shown holding an umbrella by the handle with her right hand. A bearded mugger grips her left hand by the wrist. He then freezes whilst she dexterously changes her grip to half way down the umbrella, puts it across his arm, grips the handle with her captured hand, presses it down on his wrist, and blind drunk that he is, he lets go. Then she prods him in the face with the umbrella. This truly is an example of the murderous Chinese arts that cripple an opponent. The mind marvels as it realises that only a Chinese Sifu of tremendous experience could have thought of a secret technique like that. A simpleton would never have done such a thing; she would have simply hit the attacker in the face with the umbrella in her free hand. It really makes you think.

Last and by no means least comes a magazine similar to "Secrets of Kung fu" in appearance. This was "Real Kung Fu". The first issue appeared in September 1975, and explained that although other publications on Kung Fu had tried to tell what the subject was about, "we thought we could do a better job", because they were in Hong Kong. The implication here was that people elsewhere did not understand the subject as well. Leung Ting, the Wing Chun teacher, appeared in the opening issue alongside photographs of, and with, Grandmaster Yip Man.

The Bruce Lee ingredient was a piece about Siu Kee Lun (Chan Yuen Chung), Bruce Lee and Jeet Kune Do with accompanying photographs. It was promising. Readers asked for more.

Throughout the first year of publication, articles on or by Leung Ting appeared, with either posters or shots of Bruce Lee, just to keep the pull of his name and face influencing the readership. Other articles on Kung Fu, such as Black Tiger style, Choy Lee Fut, White Crane, Hop Gar, Eagle Claw, gave people some clues about the extent of its methods and there was even the occasional reference to Karate or Taekwondo. Though at times plainly partisan in content, the magazine was obviously a thousand times more informative than the third or fourth hand stuff being churned out by the public relations style reporters abroad.

Though the latter have been criticised here, their plight was understandable. Suddenly exposed to the glare of world wide publicity through the success of Bruce Lee, the Kung Fu community itself could not accommodate the storm of enquiries and interest which burst into its previously enclosed environment. Conflicting accounts of who was who and what was what in that environment kept appearing, fuelling emotions and obscuring the facts. For example, the Wing Chun controversies following the death of Grandmaster Yip Man have dragged on for nearly twenty-five years... Sometimes there was a lull, and then the arguments would flare up again, old wounds would re-open, type writer keys would start clicking and we would be back again in the same old arena. Magazine editors in some cases added more wood to the blaze by cultivating arguments in the form of readers' letters. K.O.A. at first followed this custom, but I eventually decided against it and packed up on controversy for controversy's sake.

As had been the case when Japanese martial arts surged forward in the West in the 1960's, and subjects such as precedent and hierarchy in the martial arts had been lost on the reporters and on the sports authorities, the 'culture' of the Kung Fu world was like a whisper during an orchestral concert. Almost unheard. So if the martial arts organising bodies in western countries could not make head or tail of what was going on, small wonder that the benighted 'civilian' press and publishers were floundering.

It underlined the aspect of our media which is unable to say, 'We don't know'. It shows, contrary to the book previously referred to, that to the media, reporting is 90% a 'game'. If they don't know, they will make it up, and if they are caught out making it up, they will make a headline out of the newly discovered 'truth'. They are like the legendary Monkey king of Chinese folklore: 'The nature of Monkey is irrepressible'.

KUNG FU

In 1899, in the Shantung province of China, the little known societies of I Ho Ch'uan and Ta Tao began to make their presence felt. Because of their fighting prowess and their 'gymnastic' exercises, they were given the name of "Boxers" by the foreign missionaries and officials. This small movement soon had much popular support in its bid to throw out the "yang kuei-tzu or foreign devils.

At first, outlying mission stations were attacked and missionaries either killed or driven off. Gradually the violence spread until it reached the foreign legations at Pekin. A German Minister was killed in the street in the summer of 1899 and finally the famous seige which ended in defeat for the Boxers brought the movement in that particular form to an end.

The techniques of Kung Fu and Pa Kua have never beenindoubt as superb unarmed combat methods, as the yearly contests held in Formosa show. There is no doubt that they existed immediately before the Boxer upris ing. In his book "Village Life in China," published by Revell, 1899, the Reverend Arthur Smith wrote:

1967: we had been going one year, and knew nothing about Kung Fu. I hunted through books about missionaries and travellers in China, and managed to prise this piece out of them. It amounted to a drop in the desert compared to the deluge of the 1970's. It did have the slim virtue of on the spot observations.

"A young man whom I knew in China was set on by a number of bullies. He almost dislocated the ankle of one of them and the rest were only too glad to release him, ...

It was common to hire a number of these 'fist and foot' experts, if one's life or one's property were in danger. On one occasion a band of thieves were defeated by a group of hired unarmed combat men, an event which brings to mind the film - The Seven Samurai in which the hired samurai defend a village against brigands.

Mr. Smith saw all these 'fist and foot' men as 'bullies' or swaggerers and makes no connection between them and any religious rites. However, his experiences took place before the Boxer uprising and he may have missed at that time the growing strength of the movement.

The Boxers had some kind of religious rites, and were associated with Taoism, the ancient Chinese religion:

"Early in May, Boxer teachers came from T'ungchou, and soon we heard that a band had been organised in our town, though they were only practising in secret. Then a Taoist priest threw open his temple for their use, and soon a Boxer flag waved proudly over it."

Thus wrote Luella Miner in 1903, in her record, China's Book of Martyrs, Jennings and Pye. Another account speaks of a quarrel between two friends. One a Boxer, the other a Christian. The Boxer finally threw the latter 'high in the air.'

Kung Fu was related, it is said, to the worship of nature, and Chinese Christians were pressed to recant and bow down to 'idols.' It does seem, therefore, that with the close connection between Tai Chi Chuan and Tao and the similarity in techniques of the Boxers that these arts practised to-day in Britain, Europe, the U.S.A. and of course in the Orient, are descended from the deadly arts of the Boxers.

On the feats performed by 'fist and foot' men we quote once more from Mr. Smith's book:

"A high degree of skill in wrestling and the ability to deliver such a blow with the fist as shall knock out a brick from a wall a foot thick, are in many circumstances valuable accomplishments."

Tameshiwari - woodbreaking - and suchlike are thus no modern invention.

Bruce Lee & the Media Good Guys

Of course, not all Press reports about Bruce Lee and Kung fu were stupid or ill-informed. "Karate & Oriental Arts" and "Fighting Arts" were keeping abreast of developments, and bringing news and information to fans and martial artists in Britain. In France the magazine "Budo" was doing the same. In the United States the magazine known best to us across the Atlantic was "Black Belt", to be followed by a magazine founded by Chinese American Curtis F. Wong, with Chinese staff for the most part, with articles written by Chinese about Chinese Kung fu. It was called "Inside Kung Fu".

Later, staff and reporters and subjects in all magazines expanded in fundamental nationality as the appeal of martial arts spread across all racial boundaries. It was clear that the Japanese were keen to export their instructors, export their martial arts, export their martial arts books, export their products and their 8mm. films (no videos in those days).

The Chinese American roots stretched back into China, Taiwan and Hong Kong. There was tangible tension between those who wanted to show Chinese martial arts to foreigners, and those who wanted to keep them secret. In Britain we were for the most part dependent on importing information about these subjects but the Americans had a wealth of immigrant and American born Chinese martial artists, some of whom were glad to contribute to the growing exposed knowledge of their martial systems and chi kung (qigong) methods.

I got to hear about Curtis Wong and his new magazine "Inside Kung Fu" and wrote to buy copies to sell in England and in the K.O.A. shop. One phone call I made reminded me of the time difference between our countries when a tired voice answered my call, very politely in a laid back way, and finished the conversation by telling me that it was four o'clock in the morning. The same voice told me that they were asleep on the office floor. I imagine that no one left the offices of "Inside Kung Fu" in the early days; they were too busy keeping up with the demands of their readers.

The reticence of many Chinese martial artists, and to a much lesser extent of Japanese, gave rise to certain stories among westerners which may have an element of truth in them. This was that a Chinese martial artist would never teach a westerner correctly. It went on that if you learned from a Chinese and carried out instructions incorrectly, the teacher would nod and say that you were doing the techniques correctly. In this way the teacher did not reveal his "secrets" but was able to satisfy the endless demand from western pupils for more and more knowledge and technical expertise. Westerners were westerners, what did it matter...

Of course this did not apply to all teachers. Some were very open, and gave what they could. But yet another obstacle stood in the way of many western pupils, and this was that however much they read in books and magazines, and however much the teachers taught them, it was never enough. And it never came quickly enough. The eastern emphasis on patient learning and repetition of movements and stances, which the magazines never tired of pointing out, was something genuinely foreign in the West. We wanted to become deadly, unbeatable like the famous teachers, and above all like Bruce Lee, right now! Never mind standing in a Horse Stance for one year. We did the Horse Stance, o.k. that was it, and now what next? Many a Chinese must have shaken his head in puzzlement over his western pupils' attitudes.

Unfortunately, when the phrase associated with Bruce Lee, "the classical mess", began to be voiced, it was an open door to the students who did not want to train hard. They could point at what Bruce Lee had said as their reason. Magazines of repute stamped on this idea, but it was not registered by many students. This only goes to show that such readers read and remembered what they wanted to and not what they should have. As I said in other parts of this book, Bruce Lee put in the time, put in the hard work, and was able to demonstrate for instance his one inch punch to the martial arts public, as the martial arts media reported, but the study which went into feats of that kind was considerable.

If Lee seemed to turn his back on the "classical mess", it was surely more on the tendency in many Chinese to blindly follow a teacher or system, never questioning, never developing. This is a tendency rooted in their past, in their respect for ancestors, for tradition and for keeping in touch with what went before. When I was learning Pakua (Bagua), my teacher believed that the Sun style was the only style. It was only when I showed him a series of magazines, now no longer published, called the "Pakua Journal" that he believed there were other Pakua styles. I had told him there were, but until he saw the photographs and Chinese calligraphy in the journal, he did not believe me. In 1969 when I was learning Wu Style Tai Chi, my teacher told me that this was the only style, and that the Yang style I had already learned was not Tai Chi. The fact that Wu style had come from Yang style was something she either did not know or chose to overlook.

Such problems the magazines tried to make clear, but it took a long time, and did not convince everyone. Bruce Lee had studied a series of martial arts, some basically and thoroughly, and others more in a comparative way, that is he had looked at their principles. The panorama of Kung Fu that appeared in the early years of the publication of "Inside Kung Fu" and to a much lesser extent in "Karate & Oriental Arts" made it clear that a banquet of knowledge existed which, even if a man were to live a thousand years, he still would not have reached the end.

Lee's attitude could have only been based on looking mainly at principles. Neither he nor anyone else could possibly have examined Chinese Kung Fu as a whole and come up with a verdict about its methods.

Some of the Chinese who emerged into the glare of western interest at one end of the scale, and western martial arts madness at the other, had to deal with the situation as they saw it. If anything, to the discerning student they highlighted Bruce Lee's attitude, since they showed precisely the points made in the above paragraphs; the point about principle. The quantity, and the quality, of styles and methods made no other conclusion possible.

A striking example of the way in which styles could be brought together with no loss of face on either side, and no adverse comparisons being made, occurred in the Australian Kung fu championships in Melbourne in 1984. At this event, organised by William Cheung, a three thousand capacity crowd saw the Wing Chun expert combine with none other than Dan Inosanto in a first time ever demonstration. Both men had known Bruce Lee in different capacities. The two men gave a sparkling display of Wing Chun Butterfly Knives against Kali sticks. The classical Chinese and the Filipino rooted weapons showed what could be done when two lifetime martial artists put their brains and muscles together with nothing else in mind but "living in the zone".

For me, the most memorable lines in all the writing and reporting which followed the year 1973 were those originally written by Bruce Lee and recorded in the book, "Bruce Lee - The Man Only I Knew", by his wife Linda. They were from an essay Lee wrote as a university freshman entitled "A Moment of Understanding". They go, "...when I said I must relax, the demand for the effort in 'must' was already inconsistent with the effortlessness in 'relax'." This realisation is one which has come to other people who have gone into eastern methods and some who have for instance studied postural re-education in the West. But to find it, and other gems, amidst all the brouhaha surrounding Bruce Lee is truly gratifying. To perceive the truth of what he wrote is a big step. To be able to put it into practice is a bigger one. It is "fighting without fighting" and "doing without doing", of letting the parts designed to do something do them, and not interfering. Jeet Kune Do is translated as the Way of the Intercepting Fist. In the light of Lee's essay, a better title would have been the Way of the Not-Interfering Fist. Maybe I will start my own style using that name.

Though mentioned in the section "Media Hype", the magazines "Secrets of Kung Fu", "Real Kung Fu" and the Jafaha martial arts journal really belong in this part of the book, since more than anything else they did shed light on their subjects. Also one should mention the magazine "Fighting Arts", produced by Karate expert Terry O 'Neill in Liverpool, and the American publication "Journal of Asian Fighting Arts". Several other magazines appeared for a short time and then closed down. These included "Action Karate", "Martial Arts Movies" and a number of periodicals devoted to a particular martial art which never got anywhere because their subject matter was too limited in appeal.

Behind all such publications were not professional journalists because none of these magazines could support full time employees. They were dedicated martial artists with some ability with words, freelance writers with a martial arts interest and readers capable of writing good informative letters. In addition, the mags. gave opportunities for budding photographers, amateur and professional, to try their hand at action photography.

Some of the articles contributed to magazines were very well researched. The writers had taken great pains to obtain their information and presented it an a balanced and thoughtful way. The difficulty with Bruce Lee as a subject was to separate the rumours from the realities, the honest assessment from the partisan nonsense. Some periodicals stayed away from the star because they did not want hype in their pages, and it was only much later, when the dust had settled and the respected teachers of JKD such as Dan Inosanto could be interviewed in a calm and relaxed atmosphere that such mags. let the Bruce Lee subject in. So although Lee helped the martial arts world along to a new level of popularity, he was not welcomed as a martial arts figure by everyone.

Editors and writers who had spent years studying a martial art, flogging themselves on to more and more work, resented the fact that a young Chinese who had turned his back on much that they respected should receive such instant adulation and popularity. Of course these part time journalists had only their fellow media population to thank for this. Lee himself was as much a victim in a sense as those who felt resentment. Just as these dedicated martial artists felt pushed away from recognition by the wave of Lee's popularity, Lee himself was pushed away from his central quest by the same popularity. No one in his right mind can believe that success helped Lee as an individual. On the contrary. So, although I have not read every issue of every martial arts magazine ever published, and who has, my impression is that there are periodicals which never even mentioned his name. Likewise, there were and are martial artists who did not and do not believe his approach worthy of consideration. It is too undisciplined in the classical sense.

The phrase, "noticeable by his absence", aptly describes silence about Lee in some magazines and on the lips of some martial artists. In their eyes, he was not someone to be taken seriously. Plainly, this silence gave a balance to the hype at the other end of the scale. For the fans, for the majority, it went largely unnoticed, but for people more on the inside of the martial arts world it made a loud noise. One of the noises this silence was making could be expressed by a paraphrase of a popular song:

> He's Bruce Lee crazy,
> He's Bruce Lee mad,
> Bruce Lee has gone and robbed him
> Of the little bit of sense he had.

Of course, Bruce Lee had nothing to do with it; it was the hype. But still, this silent minority felt, and expressed it by saying nothing, that JKD was not a martial art because it had no forms, it had no defined etiquette, it had no social roots.

As editor of K.O.A. I met dozens of very famous martial artists, and hundreds if not thousands of less well known ones. Sometimes I would mention Bruce Lee to say a leading figure from Jujutsu or Karate, and would be met with a polite remark, dismissing the subject. Sometimes it would be more of a grin, and the comment, "Good for business...".

The harsh truth of course was that Bruce Lee had died, and the classical world of the martial arts would soldier on, the synthesised modern styles would continue to burgeon, flourish or die, and people would have to go to the martial arts clubs which existed, not the ones which might have done.

The irony is that out of the JKD phenomenon has come the fact that the "style" has spawned its own problems, its own rivalries and bickerings, and claims to authenticity. It emphasises the frequent appearance in history of the difference between an idea or concept and the carrying out of that idea. Supporters of JKD all support the fundamental notion of experiment and "what works", but many fall out over the meaning of this notion. True to tradition, the journalists are thus provided with ample fodder for their articles by the same problems which frequently occurred in Wing Chun, in Karate, in Jujutsu and other martial arts. If one "master" falls out with another it is good copy. If one style is described as better than another, it is good copy. If one student from a style defeats someone from another, good copy.

Maybe, in the end, the media are not to blame, it is all down to human nature.

Arrow Books of San Francisco, in 1974, published what was probably the best try in writing an account of Lee's life in the magazine format. Written by the Felix Dennis and Don Atyeo duo, "Bruce Lee, King of Kung Fu" combined photos and a solid text which must have thoroughly pleased the fans. It was rapidly gobbled up and Chinese martial artist, Brendan Lai, who featured several times in "Inside Kung Fu" magazine, was a distributor. It sold for a mere $2.50. In this publication, gone were the guesses and the outlandish, uninformed bits of journalese. The idolatry and exclamations of "ooh, aah" had disappeared too; even the layout and paper gave an impression of authority and modesty. The good guys in the background had swung into action at last.

PART FOUR

WHO MARCHED ON?

Who marched on?
Some of the 'names', since the boom days.

Since the heady days described in this book, Dan Inosanto has continued to spread the word of JKD and the martial arts of the Filipinos. Likewise, Rene Latosa has become one of the most famous teachers in the world. James DeMile expanded his teaching efforts, still maintaining the name of Wing Chun Do. Bob Breen, Bill Newman, Keith Kernspecht, Samuel Kwok, Austin Goh, and others kept the forward movement of exploration of the martial arts in motion...

It is no disrespect to say that Dan Inosanto is now an active grandfather of many young martial artists. He has taught and encouraged first generation pupils, who, in turn, have gone on to teach. He has not tried to keep pupils tied to his apron strings, and by introducing them to famous Filipino teachers and helping to organise international seminars and tournaments displayed an open attitude to knowledge and technique.

One of his first English pupils was Bob Breen. Breen was a Japanese trained Wado-ryu Karate man, as well as a student of Goju-ryu under Gogen Yamaguchi. He also dipped into Aikido. The highly formal training in Japan did not give him the spontaneous combative experience of Judo and Boxingwhich was what he was looking for, and when the Safe-T equipment pioneered by Jhoon Rhee appeared he took part in the first full contact tournaments in England.

He wrote to Dan Inosanto and at first heard nothing. Then, by a strange twist of fate he met Jay Dobrin, a telephone engineer, who had come to repair his phone. It turned out that Jay was a student of Escrima, so Bob began training with him and Bill Newman. Then the long awaited reply came from Dan Inosanto, and Bob Breen staged the first JKD/Kali seminar in England, taken by Dan. Bob and his friends were so impressed by the demonstrations given by Dan and his partner Jeff Imada that he turned around the syllabus of his Karate dojos so that training became much more free and informal.

Bob went to seminars in Los Angeles and Australia a number of times and whenever possible invited Dan to come over to England to teach. Dan introduced Bob to Tuhon Leo Gaje, to the latter's instructor/pupil Bill McGrath, and to the Canete family in the Philippines. Bob also met 'Tatung' Antonio Illustrissimo the cousin of Dan's own teacher, as well as Ondo Caburnay of the Arnis de Abaniko style. Bob and other Escrima students formed the World Escrima Kali Arnis Federation and in 1989 the first World championships took place in Cebu Philippines. He went on to train and captain English Escrima teams which did well in this and similar events. By 1994, he grew tired of taking part in competitions and returned to studying the arts in a more traditional manner. His club in London is always up to full strength, and can be said to be on the 'cutting edge' of martial arts training. The basis of training is a combination of Kickboxing, Thai, Filipino and Bruce Lee Jun fan Kickboxing. In addition, various trapping and locking techniques are studied, along with stick and knife training. Bob himself continues to investigate any new and effective martial art which appears, such as the grappling methods which have grabbed the headlines over the last few years.

Rene Latosa came to England as a young United States airman in the 1970's. He had been taught by Angel Cabales, Leo Giron, Dentoy Revilar, Maximo Sarmiento and by his own father, John Latosa. The Latosa-Escrima system and the organistion which promotes it is said to be the largest in the world today. This is down to the hard work of Rene himself, his close students Bill Newman and Brian Jones - instructors in their own right - and the first rate help in Europe of German martial artist Keith Kernspecht, himself a long time student of Wing Chun. Bill Newman, 9th level, has also been investigating mediaeval weapons through his knowledge of Escrima. All the leading teachers of the system are kept busy travelling and passing on their methods to the many student members around the globe.

Larry Hartsell is a first generation student of Bruce Lee's from the 1970's. He was one of the Los Angeles Chinatown Group. He continued to study with Guro Dan Inosanto, meeting on a weekly basis, sometimes more. These weekly workouts have continued for about thirty years! Larry points out that they are both busy men, conducting seminars every weekend and doing international tours four times a year. He teaches privately and has an Intensive Training Programme.

Larry Hartsell was a close friend of Brandon Lee and the two worked together. Larry reflects that, "I found him to be much unlike his father. He once told me that he wanted to be known as an individual. He had great skills as a martial artist and went in his own direction both in the movies and his personal life. He was truly an amazing person and I cared for him deeply." Hartsell's association, the Jun Fan Jeet Kune Do Grappling Association has worldwide representatives. It thrives because it is composed of 'dedicated individuals' who are committed to the promotion and perpetuation of the art. In preparing this book, it was noticeable that people in the field are dedicated. It may be that this stems in part from the inspiration of Bruce Lee, and also that students feel that even though they are being taught, they are at the same time developing their 'own thing'. It is a community of individuals.

Hartsell stresses that people have sometimes one side of themselves which is stronger than another side. They all contribute: something spiritual, something physical, something scientific. He says, 'Working together will benefit everyone and consequently the general public and future generations'. The spirit of the association comes from Bruce Lee's own words: 'Use no way as way, have no limitation as limitation'. Obviously echoing the spirit of the Taoists and Zen Buddhists. A careful check is kept on students, and even when they qualify and receive their awards or level degrees they have to attend at least two seminars per year taken either by Guro Dan Inosanto or Larry Hartsell himself. This ensures the maintenance of standards, and is a very good idea. Each level takes one year of training minimum. The levels are:

Beginning/Intermediate/Advanced/Apprentice Instructor/Associate Instructor and finally Full Instructor

K.O.A. no. 124 for February 1987 featured Larry Hartsell, in an article written by Terry Barnett and Debbie Kirkham, photos by Greg Rhodes. The latter was omnipresent when JKD visitors were around. The same issue had a two page piece about the "Media Muck Rake" which dealt with a programme being made by a TV company on the use of weapons in martial arts clubs. They were attempting to criticise and blow the scene out of all proportion as usual, and in an interview with me, the chief reporter of the TV crew made the never to be forgotten statement about martial arts and weapons: 'I DON'T KNOW ANYTHING ABOUT IT AT ALL!' Obviously she was just the right person for the job!

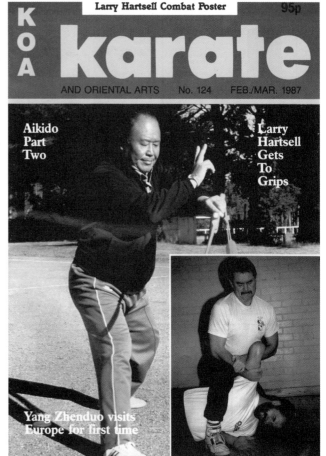

James DeMile developed other martial arts related programmes in addition to his JKD and Wing Chun Do activities. One of these is the DeMile Law Enforcement Defensive Tactics Programme for the police, military, executives and government organisations. The harsher side of life was one of his earliest discoveries, as he was brought up in an orphanage for twelve years where the law was 'survival of the fittest'. His achievements outside the Bruce Lee field included being Undefeated U.S. Air Force heavyweight boxing champion for two years, hand to hand combat instructor for the Green Berets, First Special Forces Group at Fort Lewis in 1985 and 1986, and teaching different weapons skills to the FBI and Secret Service, plus appearances in seminars at police academies across the United States. He is also a Deputy Sheriff of the state of Ohio.

He has been inducted into the prestigious World Martial Arts Hall of Fame. Recognition in areas too numerous to mention make him a leading martial arts figure. He has produced some ingenious spring loaded dummies to aid in training which give immediate feedback to the student. These and other feedback processes can build up reflex speed to an extent that a 60 year old can equal or better that of a 20 year old. All in all, DeMile has expanded on a wider front than most other teachers, which merely underlines the old saying, to each his own.

Bob Breen (l) training with Guro Dan Inosanto. The looks on the faces say it all. Warmth, respect, enjoyment, interest, awareness... What better atmosphere for studying martial arts. Photo : Norma Harvey

Above: Larry Hartsell pulls Terry Barnett on to a straight punch.
Photo : Greg Rhodes

WRIST & STEEL

I referred already to films with fencing sequences. In researching this book I spoke to Bob Anderson, (see chapter "Blades of the West"). This former British Olympic fencing coach has been swordmaster in a number of films, including 'By The Sword' and the recent swash-buckler 'Zorro'. Anderson replied interestingly when I spoke about the wrist touching sequence in 'By The Sword' and the similarity of its basic premise to that of Chi Sao of Wing Chun and Push Hands of Tai Chi. I told him about Bruce Lee's expeditions into similar subjects which centred on the subject of sensitivity. The memorable wrist touching scenes in "Enter the Dragon" spring to mind. Anderson explained that the fencing method is usually expressed in French, because they have been especially focussed on the subject. The expression is 'Sentiment du Fer", which means literally 'feeling of the iron' and more aptly 'sensitivity to the steel'. In the weaponless train-ing exercise it is a question of sensitivity to the wrist of your partner, providing an indication of what he or she is doing, and may be about to do.

He said that in modern fencing, the emphasis had long ago shifted from interest in that traditional type of subject, to simply scoring a point, and to a more athletic approach. This subject was referred to by other fencers I spoke to. As former editor of K.O.A. this was striking because Karate underwent a similar transition to point scoring 'Sport Karate' and in fact this competitive tournament side of martial arts also came into prominence years back. But just as there remains a solid core of traditionalists in martial arts, so a core of fencing enthu-siasts have retained and are developing a focus on traditional old school ideas about the importance of sensitivity to blade pressure and similar methods. Anderson mentioned Scotland and France in this connection.

So interesting it is to see this type of parallel process in worlds which have similarities in content, but are continents and centuries apart.

Jun Fan Jeet Kune Do is an organisation of individuals who got together in Seattle, where Bruce Lee is buried, in 1996, at the invitation of Linda Lee Cadwell. It consisted of prestigious martial artists who were pupils of Bruce Lee. Among its aims were to keep people informed about the philosophy, methods and ideas of Bruce Lee on an on going basis, and to show that everyone who studies should think of reaching a point where he or she can express themselves through what is suitable for them and reject what is unsuitable. The group referred to themselves as the Nucleus.

Its declared goals consist of a series of steps which will ensure a clear understanding of Jun Fan Jeet Kune Do, to maintain standards and to call upon students and teachers to uphold a code of ethics. The name itself came from a realisation that Jun Fan Gung Fu and Jeet Kune Do cannot be kept apart from one another. Among the Charter members of the organisation were: Linda Lee Cadwell, Taky Kimura, Richard Bustillo, Larry Hartsell, Dan Inosanto, Daniel Lee and Ted Wong. Their Information Network gives an impression of a group of people who wish on the one hand to achieve their goals and at the same time do not want to judge others and interfere in others' goals.

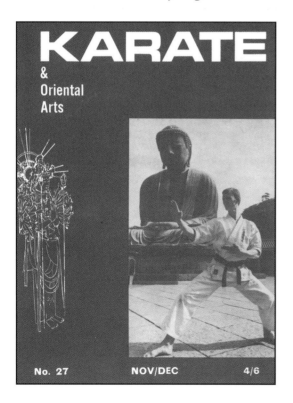

In KOA no. 27 we featured Brian Waites. Though a student of Karate, Waites had tried Kickboxing in Japan, where such contests were all the rage.

Like Bob Breen, Waites found that exposure to another fighting art very much broadened his horizons and raised many new questions.

For instance individuals may be 'recognised' for their abilities, etc., but this 'recognition' is not the 'equivalent of a licence' to teach JFJKD.

I had heard on the grapevine that Dan Inosanto had distanced himself from the JFJKD group because he "wanted to do his own thing". This is acknowledged by the Nucleus's own words, but they say that their regard for Inosanto is just as high as it ever was. The tone suggests that the parting was amicable and understood on both sides. In any event, some of the Nucleus members themselves were originally certified by Dan. Most organisations, inside or outside the martial arts world, undergo change, and this one is no exception. One speculates that the Nucleus had and has some kind of mutual 'feel' for what is wanted, and it may be this is more than a set or rules or resolutions which guide them.

There are quite a number of others in different parts of the world who carry the banner of Bruce Lee's ideas. No judgement of them on my part is feasible, as I do not have the necessary information. But to quote a saying from one of my own teachers, "Wherever you get people, you get what people do" is the most diplomatic way to speak about people whom you do not know. It is an excellent rule of thumb. From my own experience of martial arts, which covers over fifty years, you have to see what people are teaching, use your own common sense, and stay with them or simply leave. "Absorb what is useful"! (Dan Inosanto)

THE JEET KUNE DO SYMBOL

The symbol used in JKD is based on the ancient Chinese Yin-Yang image, whose date of origin is difficult to determine. The symbol we have today is sometimes compared to an egg, the white corresponding to the Yang and the yolk to the Yin, male and female, active and passive. The gradual decrease in the width of white and the growing width of black indicates that as one force weakens the other grows stronger. The symbol is also compared to two fish, lying head to tail.

The respected Chinese philosopher and academician Fung Yu-Lan says in his book "A Short History of Chinese Philosophy", Free Press, 1966 that the symbol used today was devised by Chou Tun-Yi, the "first cosmological philosopher" in the 11th century C.E.(A.D.). Chou came into possession of some mystic diagrams produced by early Taoist mystics who regarded them as keys to the attainment of longevity. Chou modified them and produced the new symbol. This was not done arbitrarily, but was meant to illustrate certain aspects of the I-Ching or Book of Changes.

As is common knowledge, the symbol today is usually associated in martial arts with Tai Chi Chuan, more than with any other art. So, apart from the fact that Bruce Lee studied Tai Chi for a while when he was a youngster, it is superficially surprising that he used a modified Yin-Yang symbol to represent his experimental Jeet Kune Do art. Apart from the original symbol's well known meanings, which can be read into the JKD symbol, the fact that it has 'projections' or arrows taking energy away from or going around the central symbol is probably more or equally significant.

The signifiance could be extensively interpreted, but the most obvious is as follows. The basic symbol represents the classical, traditional methods, and the peripheral circling projections can represent exploration or experiment into what is not classical or traditional. Each traditional Chinese Kung Fu style usually centres around one factor. This could be an animal as in Crane style, or a type of energy such as the linear energy of Hsing-I or the circular energy of Pakua, or the direct forward energy of Wing Chun. Or it could be an emphasis on technique such as the distinct seizing methods of Chin-Na. Whatever factor you choose, it is distinctly true that classical styles are usually circumscribed and in a sense closed systems. The exceptions to this finding are where a martial artist learns more than one style and eventually amalgamates two or more of them into another style, such as Sun Style Tai Chi of Sun Lu-Tang.

Sun was a Pakua and Hsing-I master. His Tai Chi style contains rippling or following steps which could have originated in either of the two former styles, and also back arching movements possibly coming from Hsing-I. But even though his style comes from a mixture of classical styles, in turn his own Sun Tai Chi has become in a sense a new 'classical' style, modified only by the requirements of competitive performance Tai Chi events. So even the synthesised styles of later generations of classical martial artists do not essentially fall within the experimental approach of JKD. They represent examples of a sort of natural development in the martial arts, rather than a deliberate underlying approach of "absorb what is useful", to quote Dan Inosanto. No student of Sun style for example would learn it with the express intention of looking for what works and throwing away what does not.

Another important consideration when looking at symbols which represent something mobile and alive is to remember that that is just what they are. They are moving. This is something I registered decades ago, and it helps. If you imagine the JKD symbol like a Catherine Wheel firework which spins around its axis giving off a jet of flame and energy at the perimeter then you have some notion of what is meant. In the symbol there is no apparent centre, but as it is circular there is indeed a centre. Imagine then that it rotates, and that the projections or arrow are like the firework energy output. These are the exploratory efforts of the student into what works, moving outside the classical boundaries. The centre can represent at least two things: the classical basis, the original art that any martial artist studied, and the generation of energy from the student's own body and psyche. The philosophical and practical implications are great. They simply underline the potential in Bruce Lee's martial arts approach.

A further interpretation of the JKD symbol is to see it not as a projection away from the centre, but as a movement around and perhaps towards the centre. This can be seen as a student's circling of the essential Yin-Yang principle, learning from it, receiving from it, and attempting to go to the centre of it. The fact that the circling arrows are one Yin and one Yang represents the phases and energies of the student and his quest. Without too much intellectual sweat one can make a comparison between the underlying theme of "Silent Flute" and the JKD symbol. Cord searches for his goal, Carradine's flute man undergoes successive transformations each time he is defeated by Cord, the hero's spirits rise and fall, and finally he sees that he is really searching for himself. His struggle, as traditional "Ways" indicate, is with his own nature. Whether he tries to escape from his centre, or reach his centre, the outcome is the same. So the symbol is once more like a finger pointing at the moon.

YIN YANG SYMBOL

JEET KUNE DO SYMBOL

BRUCE LEE'S POWER PUNCH & JAMES W. DeMILE

"To my knowledge, I am one of the few people to whom Bruce Lee ever taught the Power Punch..."

~~~~~~~~~~~~~~~~~~~~~~~~~~~~

In one of Bruce Lee's many demonstrations of his skills, a tough street wise man, considerably heavier than he was, came up on stage to trade techniques with him. The man was confident that he could deal with the 140 lb. Chinese who was holding American audiences spellbound with his lithe movements and amazing speed. Used to street fighting, the man threw a punch at Bruce, which was easily dealt with. Successive attacks were treated in the same way. Finally, Bruce gave his opponent a gentle tap on the head, proving that if he wanted he could knock him out. The American gracefully accepted that he had been beaten by a superior martial artist and later the same day struck up a friendship.

Thus, James DeMile became one of Bruce Lee's first pupils in the early 1960's. In the 1970's we began importing books from him, which he had written under the general title of "Tao of Wing Chun Do", the Way of Wing Chun. They acknowledged a certain debt to Bruce Lee and traditional Wing Chun but set out to present the art in a different way based on the author's own understanding. In addition, DeMile produced a book called "Bruce Lee's 1 and 3 inch Power Punch." A very slim booklet it was really, and aimed to present Lee's own, till then, secret Power Punch. DeMile wrote in the introduction,

"To my knowledge, I am one of the few people to whom Bruce Lee ever taught the Power Punch, not because it is difficult to do, but simply because Bruce wanted to keep it an exclusive technique." DeMile goes on to explain that he feels that it should be explained to everyone, particularly those who did not want to spend time doing martial arts training. In the book it is pointed out that mental preparation is necessary, and instructions are given for a limited but essential number of arm and wrist exercises. Fundamentally, the effectiveness of the very short range punching explained in the book depends on four things. These are:

    a. mental focus
    b. good relaxation
    c. rapid movement from relaxation to tension
    d. correct use of body weight

This of course applies to many physical actions, such as cracking a whip, hitting a nail with a hammer head and so on. The point is though, that unless a person is particularly talented, it does require a lot of training, along the lines of the four points above, to bring about a powerful punch from a range of one or two or three inches away. The fact is that it can be done. Having spent a little time on it myself, purely for the purpose of being able to give a verdict in this book, it would seem that the punch delivers shocking power, rather than smashing through or battering ram power. One can easily imagine Bruce Lee investigating punching and coming to the type of conclusions explained by James DeMile in his little book. The original question about a punch which travels merely a few inches would be: How to harness body weight and speed to the best effect?

If the body "fell" forwards on to the front foot, it was prevented from falling by the front foot landing, but also by the opponent's body getting in the way of the fist. Jack Dempsey, the former heavyweight boxing champion of the world wrote a book in which he described a "falling punch". Basically this involved "falling" forward and using the punching arm like a battering ram, with as much of the body weight as possible behind it. Speed would come from the launch from feet and legs, and as the body "fell" its weight would be prevented from falling by the combined effect of the front leg landing and the fist hitting the opponent. In a somewhat similar way, James DeMile explains Bruce Lee's notion of the Power Punch, in which if you are punching with your right fist, to the body, you let your weight sink, moving the centre of gravity over the left leg, and your "fall" is stopped either by your opponent's body or a punch bag or, when training alone without

(Below: shot of James Demile's weapons and training room - K.O.A. April 1977)

apparatus, by the contraction of your left leg muscles. In any case, there is a strong element of "falling".

When an object falls from a surface or is launched from a surface, it begins to fall at once, and all its weight is behind that fall. In the case of a person, the fall is improved if the person is relaxed, so that he or she can add to the effect of gravity with muscle power. So, the study of short or long range punching is a very interesting one and can lead to many more useful questions, such as: How is power best generated over a given distance? Body weight is already provided, free of charge so to speak. Relaxation is essential for fast mobilisation... And so on... As everyone knows, Bruce Lee appeared at a martial arts tournament in California and demonstrated his explosive short range punch on a big Karate-ka, sent him flying and then it was bees around a honey pot to learn the secret. But what of Wing Chun Do?

From a number of points of view, Wing Chun Do is most interesting when it deals with Chi Sao. Chi Sao became known largely through the Wing Chun system of Kung Fu. It is a training method in which partners keep their arms in contact and push-punch at very close range, and by pressure and body movement "parry" the blows whilst still maintaining arm contact. You have to do it to appreciate it, and I had had a taste with Rolf Clausnitzer, Greco Wong and William Cheung, though I never was drawn to focus on Wing Chun itself. The purpose is to develop "sensitivity", meaning that you become familiar with being in contact with an opponent in the "tangle" that sometimes occurs when you are fighting close. You can sense where he is moving and where his weight is and so forth. Hawkins Cheung, a Wing Chun brother of Bruce Lee's, was interviewed about the art and spoke with respect of Yip Man's amazing abilities in Chi Sao.

Why this particular exercise is so interesting is because it touches on many sides of martial arts. It touches on the searching for grips in Judo, on the melee of arms which occurs when Karate-ka get very close, on the grabbing for a grip in Aikido and on the Push Hands training of Tai Chi. It is an excellent training aid for any martial artist.

What James DeMile presents in his book is a very simple analysis of the energy and balance aspects of Chi Sao, from his own perspective, his Wing Chun Do perspective. Where Bruce Lee is

Bruce Lee's first public demo of his Power Punch made the martial arts world sit up and take notice... after a big Karate-ka had "sat down".

reported to have been a teacher who expected his pupils to catch on quick, DeMile goes a more western route, taking the method apart so that an absolute beginner can begin to see what is involved, and why. He takes the simple approach of demonstrating the positive or advantageous parts of an attack, for instance a strong push, and then the negative parts. So for instance if you push, your opponent may lose his balance, but on the other hand you may lose yours; the same with pulling. This approach may seem laboured to some martial artists who prefer a more lively, living attitude, but for a large percentage of students it is more comprehensible. Furthermore, as a student begins to understand the importance of balance, he prepares himself or herself for a better understanding of the power punch. The latter depends very much on correct or rather appropriate tensions in the legs and lower torso and this in turn is a matter of fundamental balance. Using DeMile's own example, it is no use being able to generate force over a short distance if you lose your balance in the process.

As a student gets to grips with basic balance, he is led to see that balance is affected by every movement he makes. This is obvious when you see it in black and white print, but when you are faced with an opponent or partner and your hands and arms meet, it becomes at first much less obvious. Your shoulders tend to hunch up, your arms tense up and you can easily lose your balance. DeMile shows how to take impact, pressure, force and so on, whilst retaining balance by adjusting to the incoming energies.

Gradually, a student will see more and more clearly the relationship between movement and balance, so that for example he will realise that if he holds his arms too high his balance will be affected and the efficiency of his Chi Sao. He will notice that there is a definite relationship too between the upper body and the lower body and legs. To a martial artist, such things are the staff of life. They are the food which keeps his art alive and interesting.

Considering James DeMile's build, compared with that of Bruce Lee, it is easy to see that although he was Lee's pupil it was inevitable that he should find his own route into what he learned. A pupil cannot become his teacher. He learns from him and then with application must find his own "style", if that is the right word. That said, it is clear that DeMile learned important things from Bruce Lee, and has succeded in doing his own thing in the matter of JKD. Physique, martial arts background, upbringing and so on, all con-

If you push,

your

opponent

may lose

his

balance,

but...

you may

lose

yours...

balance is

affected by

every

movement

he makes.

tribute to what a martial artist becomes. JKD approaches can be the inspiration to bring all this together.This is perhaps one of the big differences between JKD and traditional martial arts. The latter has a limited, though maybe very large, number of techniques. It has a syllabus, much like a university or college syllabus. As you go through the syllabus your grade or position within the system rises. You can be graded or take exams, and in theory you are better than the people who are lower down the scale. But this is not an infallible method. You may be skilful in the syllabus but not very able to apply what you have learned to fighting. If you are a Karate man you may be very effective against another Karate man but not good against a wrestler. This situation is encouraged because the techniques you learn are based on defending or attacking with someone who does the same thing as you do. It does not always take this into account.

JKD on the other hand has a different set of principles based on approaching a contest through adaptation. It is not so much a question of, if you do this then I do that, but rather so to speak keeping an open mind and being able to respond.

On the other hand, not everyone is able to improvise, to respond from the wisdom of the body, as it were. And this is where set routines and forms and pre-arranged sparring, such as we find in Karate, traditional Kung Fu and other martial arts come into their own. If anyone were ever a "natural" it must have been Bruce Lee; but not everyone is a natural. They need the fundamentals of tradition to start them off. A classically taught boxer will be taught to lead with his left, keep his right up, tuck his chin away, move, weave, etc. Later he may throw all this away, do his own thing, but he does not start with that.

James DeMile approaches Wing Chun Do from this perspective. He may, like many instructors, have started his teaching career with a different perspective, but harsh experience of the limitations, as well as the talents, of beginners may have changed his approach. His book leads students from one context to another, so that by the final page a lot of preparatory ground has been covered. My own view is that Bruce Lee, DeMile's mentor, would not have been disappointed in his pupil's work. Since these early days, the latter has extended and deepened his study and teaching of martial arts.

If anyone were ever a 'natural' it must have been Bruce Lee. But not everyone is a natural. They need the building bricks of of tradition to start them off.

JEET KUNE DO SEMINAR

An opportunity to learn the training methods and concepts of the late **BRUCE LEE**

LARRY HARTSELL
One of Bruce Lee's original students
Ten years in law enforcement
Black Belt in Kenpo Karate under Ed Parker
Recently Mr. T's bodyguard

LONDON

SATURDAY 31st OCTOBER
SUNDAY 1st NOVEMBER

SEMINARS ARE OPEN TO ALL MARTIAL ARTISTS REGARDLESS OF PREVIOUS EXPERIENCE. DESIGNED TO COMPLEMENT, NOT CONFLICT WITH YOUR CURRENT STYLE. COME EXPLORE THE MARTIAL ARTS - JKD, PHILIPPINO KALI AND ESCRIMA, BOXING, EDGED WEAPONS, AND EXECUTIVE SECURITY. CONTACT NINO BERNARDO FOR OTHER SEMINAR LOCATIONS

LARRY HARTSELL
JEET KUNE DO
CONCEPTS

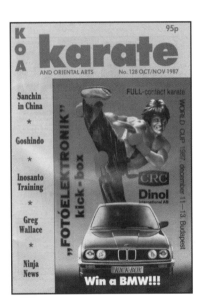

Nino Bernardo invited several JKD teachers to his well known training centre in North London. In KOA no. 128 was a long report of an interview with Dan Inosanto in which Dan recalled an incident in which someone had said to the star, "You can't combine Jujutsu and Wing Chun". Swiftly Lee did so, and added, "I just did!"

The same issue contained an article about the connection between Sanchin Kata of Okinawan Goju Karate, its applications and Chinese Kung Fu. This was courtesy of Garry Malone and Shihan Morio Higaonna, the thinking man's Sensei.

News of topless women kickboxing events also filtered through into this issue. No pics... Jhoon Rhee figuratively stamped on the camera!

Note: Among the K.O.A. memorabilia are two photocopied sheets sent to us by James DeMile. They are both from Bruce Lee's book, "Chinese Gung Fu: the Philosophical Art of Self Defense". They show photographs taken in 1962. One is of DeMile standing beside Jesse Glover, and DeMile has pencilled in:" Jesse Glover, Bruce's original student (on the left) and first assistant instructor." Then there is a photograph of Bruce Lee himself from DeMile's private collection. The second sheet shows Lee in action against two attackers and DeMile arrows in on himself with the comment, "When I was young, without beard." Somehow these two faded sheets convey more than all the film stills put together.

Archive photo from KOA No 76, January1979 showing:
 (l. to r.):

Bill Newman, Keith Kernspecht, Leung Ting and Rene Latosa beneath a photo of Grandmaster Yip Man. Kernspecht's martial arts club was housed in a German castle and promoted Wing Chun and the Filipino arts. His burly frame and black beard gave him an almost piratical appearance, but was perhaps more appropriately reminiscent of the Teutonic Knights of his own country.

Latosa, Newman and Kernspecht later expanded their enterprise into a world wide network of clubs, with thousands of members.

> "Who can make muddy water clear? The sage..."
>
> (from the writings of Lao-tze)

The Great Big German Rrrip-off The Tao!

THE STIRRER WAS "IN STIR"

This is a true story. It happened in 1977 and the photostats of the documents involved are in the hands of KOA magazine. The originals are in the hands of well-known personalities of the martial arts world.

Once upon a time there was a man. He lived in Germany. West Germany to be precise. One day, as he was sitting in his cell, yes, he was in stir, he thought that he could not carry on his favourite pastime, making money, in the usual way. and this made him very unhappy. He was a regular reader of all kinds of books and magazines and he began to notice that there were a lot of people all over Europe who were interested in martial arts. One fine morning he had an idea. " I will get someone to put an advertisement in a magazine of martial arts. This advertisement of mine will not be about your average Wado-ryu or Shotokan karate course. No, my advertisement will be worded in such a way that when people read it, not only will they be convinced that mine is no ordinary course, but they will believe that after attending it they will be able to make themselves invisible like a Ninja and that they will be able to breathe real fire and brimstone like the legendary Chinese dragon!"

This cunning and completely-without-scruple man continued to reflect in this way for many days. His life in the prison was not very exciting and the prospect of pulling off such a coup tickled his fancy.

We are not certain at this stage how Mr. X placed his advertisement; certainly the magazine that accepted it did not check up on him; nor, we must assume, did the prison authorities know anything about his imaginative scheme. So, into the clean water of the stream of martial arts this prisoner in a German prison had begun to pour large dollups ot mud. And who, at that stage. could make it clear? Who indeed?

A PHYSICIAN CAN'T CURE IN HIS OWN COUNTRY?

Our unscrupulous prisoner was also a reader of the Christian New Testament. He knew from his reading that people are not easily convinced of the qualifications of someone who comes from their own country. So, in deciding on the name of the instructor or instructors who would conduct this fabulous martial arts course of his he decided to choose someone from another country. He therefore christened the instructor of the course, Sifu T. L. Cheong. (Of course, no one who has the name of T. L. Cheong has anything to do with this story). And for good measure he threw in the name of Mr. Jan Wright. (who appears elsewhere in this magazine), and Mr. James Demile who also appears.

Mr. Wright and Mr. Demile at this stage thought that Mr. X was a steady, hard-working martial artist, living and working in West Germany and behaving in every respect as befits a martial arts teacher.

HANDS ACROSS THE SEA

To get the ball rolling, Mr. X wrote to James Demile and invited him to come and teach on the course in various European countries. He also wrote to Mr. Wright and a flow of letters to and fro across the English Channel and the Atlantic ocean soon had everyone concerned in the right mood for the Big German Rrrrip-Off!

According to our information, pretty soon the kind of paper that was moving across the Channel, and through the mail bags of Europe, had changed from little black marks on white paper to elaborate green marks or blue or brown marks on crisp, off-white paper, with a thin sliver of wire running through it; also, there would be a picture of the Queen of England on the paper, or some famous European statesman. Mr. X kept stashing this new kind of paper away somewhere and writing down in his mind how much of this paper he had. Where he put it, no one knows.

COUNT DOWN

Time was passing. Mr. Demile bought his air ticket to Germany. Mr. Wright prepared to travel south. All over Europe, students whose bank balances were lighter by this time packed their bags. From Yorkshire, from Austria, from France and points West, the caravan moved in towards Mannheim, West Germany. Wing Chun, Hapkido, Chi Sau Tao, Chi Tao San, Dim Mak, Dim Huk, Tai Chi, and Uncle Tom Cobley and all would be taught on this course of a lifetime.

"THE SAGE CONVEYS INSTRUCTION WITHOUT WORDS" (Tao Te Ching)

The truth of this statement was soon borne in upon Mr. Demile when he arrived at his destination. We quote:
" I arrived in Frankfurt August 8th and went to Mannheim directly. You can imagine my shock and disappointment to find that Mr. K was a convict. I asked to visit with him and he refused to see me. I called Austria to confirm the programme and found that it also was not true." Daily, students arrived in Mannheim, only to find, to quote once more from the Tao Te Ching:
" Conveying lessons without words, reaping profit without action - there are few in the world who can attain to this!" The bleak, silent walls of Mannheim prison fulfilled these aspirations of the Chinese Sage to a T! Back, back across the unsympathetic railway lines of Frankfurt went the unfortunate martial arts students, their lives saddened but perhaps much wiser through the efforts of a Chinese Sage and a German convict.

There was no course, there never had been!

A WARNING

The story that we have related above comes from Mr. Wright, Mr. Demile; and Mr. Kernspecht of Wing Tsun fame. Other people have telephoned KOA magazine about it. Mr. Velte, a West German martial arts supplier is co-operating by informing all martial arts magazines in Europe about the con trick or rip-off, which has been perpetrated.

As KOA magazine have no conclusive evidence that the name of the man who carried out the rip-off is correct, we have not printed it; but, the name begins with K and has six letters in it. The moral of the true story is to trust no advertisements for courses in martial arts unless you can be absolutely sure about the credentials of the person who is advertising. This can be done in a number of ways, and it does not require a lot of intelligence to think of them. As far as Britain is concerned, KOA magazine find that the creation of the Martial Arts Commission and its continued existence is the best type of antidote to this kind of thing. The same applies when sending off for courses and goods from martial arts suppliers. If in doubt, ask for the items you want to be sent CASH ON DELIVERY; then you can examine the goods and if it is a con-trick, tell the Post Office immediately and get your money back. The Post Office will also be in a position to put the conmen out of business if your complaint is justified. As for all the unfortunate people who went to Germany and Mr. Demile who came from the U.S.A., we can only extend our sincere sympathy. Perhaps their unwelcome experiences will at least serve to warn others of the pitfalls that lurk in the martial arts world.

OFFICIAL ACTION

Letters have been sent to German Embassies about this affair, but basing our opinion on past experience, it is unlikely that anyone will re-coup the losses even if full proof of guilt is found. Nowadays the law where cash is concerned is very difficult to enforce. We end with another quotation from the Tao Te Ching:
"The struggle for rare possessions drives a man to actions injurious to himself."

CALENDAR OF A CON:

1. *PLACE AN ADVERTISEMENT FOR A COURSE WHICH WILL TEACH PEOPLE HOW TO FLY.*

2. *USE A CHINESE NAME AND THE NAMES OF A FEW WELL KNOWN MARTIAL ARTISTS.*

3. *FIND AN ACCOMPLICE WHO IS DIFFICULT TO TRACE.*

4. *CARRY ON LENGTHY AND CONVINCING CORRESPONDENCE.*

5. *PUT THE FEES FOR THE COURSE IN A SAFE PLACE.*

6. *GO TO JAIL, DIRECTLY TO JAIL, BUT COLLECT 10,000 MARKS AS YOU PASS "GO".*

7. *STAY IN JAIL UNTIL EVERYONE HAS GONE BACK HOME.*

8. *COME OUT OF JAIL AND COLLECT 10,000 MARKS.*

INNER LESSONS OF CHOW GAR

Grandmaster Ip Shui, with his son C. K. Ip behind him.
Paul Whitrod on left.

Master Paul Whitrod has been teaching Chow Gar Praying Mantis in London for three years now, ever since he came back from Hong Kong in March, 1981. Whilst in Hong Kong he lived with his Grandmaster Ip Shui, head of the Chow Gar Praying Mantis style. Paul's Master is the Grandmaster's son, C.K. Ip, who came to London in the early 70's. Paul began his training through C.K. Ip, who eventually returned to Hong Kong. Paul did not leave it at that, he followed his Master in 1979 to Hong Kong and was lucky enough to stay in his Master's Father's home, Grandmaster Ip Shui, where he was treated like their own son.

Paul was taught personally by the Grandmaster and his Master and found this to be a unique experience, practising five hours a day and absorbing all that he could about Chow Gar Praying Mantis.

The Grandmaster gave Paul his permission to teach this style in England, and in honour of this Paul received the Lau Soei photograph, as well as a photograph of the Grandmaster and his Master, and a certificate of approval on completion of this style and bonesetting medicine.

Whilst in Hong Kong Paul had to kneel in front of the Lau Soei photograph, and also knelt before the Grandmaster and his Master, to become an inside student, one of only five accepted (four within his own family). This was done to show Paul's honour and loyalty to the style.

They chose Paul because of his character and understanding of the Chow Gar Praying Mantis style. It was a sad departure when Paul left Hong Kong. Their family, Sons, and Son-in-Law came to Tai Kak Airport to see Paul leave in March 1981. Paul returned to Hong Kong in December, 1982, when he studied Chinese medicine, and returned again with his students in August this year (1984).

ABOUT CHOW GAR PRAYING MANTIS KUNG FU
Master Paul Whitrod is the 6th generation of practitioners from the founder Chow An Naam. Chow Gar Praying Mantis centres its ideas to make one understand about your body and its development. We exercise the joints, tendons, ligaments and bones, as well as the practice of the Hay Gun (Air Power).

The body is divided into nine parts, each part has a certain exercise thus enabling to feel that area, so in time you can move your body in one piece smoothly. You have to build up a density feeling in your body, that is why so much emphasis is placed on the traditional exercise and the first form (SaamBoJin), this produces the shock power.

We do not use weights or wooden dummies, because this creates a dead feeling in your arms, secondly you cannot absorb or divert power.

Chow Gar Praying Mantis is an offensive art and a defensive, incorporating straight and circular movements. One particular form named Bo Sim Kuen (catching the insect), consists of catching, seizing and holding. Another form Num Gen Tong Long (power of the Praying Mantis) helps to produce the explosive power. But these are only techniques. The truth of this style is in the raw existence of its methods of training to develop a firm foundation. As Paul explains without this nothing can be achieved.

Practically all the forms in Chow's Family Praying Mantis have three stages, based on the development of Gung Lik. Inch Force can be achieved through this style, not just from the fist but from every part of the body.

To help you to understand this, one form called "Gen Tung Gen" will produce power shock strength, provided the basics such as Chia Sau, Doei Chong, arm and breathing exercises "Hay Gung" are done well and digested.

All the techniques in this style are direct, fast and simple. Your power should come out like lightning, and is referred to as Hanging Power, snapping tight like the jerk of a noose. The Five Elements of Metal, Wood, Water, Fire and Earth are important aspects of this style, especially in the Air Power, Hay Gung. This helps you to understand the Five Big Strength and Five Small Strength aspects when fighting. Yin and Yang philosophy also play a part in the style of course, since it is neither a hard nor soft style but a mixture.

MEDICINE
Grandmaster Ip Shui and his son C.K. Ip taught Paul their Bonesetter Medicine which consists of mixing certain herbal preparations for broken bones, torn ligaments, internal injuries, bruises, etc., and most good Kung fu men study this side of things.

WAFU – BUDDHIST SPIRITUAL MEDICINE – SUNG GUNG
This Paul found great difficulty in understanding and it will take years of hard study to make it work. The idea is to call the twenty three spirits of the past to heal the sick person. Chinese characters are drawn on the patient with two fingers, then with a brush, dipping it into water which has the Buddha's blessing.

Also, the characters must be written in the incense which is burned at the same time. Paul witnessed a person who could not walk gradually being cured over a period of one month. The name and address of this person is available.

Paul received a diploma in his successful studies from the school, and now teaches in London. Tel: 01-552-7631.

On guard prepared to attack.

Press in to sense opponent's power.

Sharply claw his extended bridge arm down and attack with cutting forearm, Pai Sau. The 'going in' power is a must in Chow Family Praying Mantis.

*

During the boom days, all types of Chinese scrolls, pictures and posters were in vogue. Above is one which was very popular, showing an eagle and tiger, echoing the names of Kung Fu styles and techniques.

KOA no. 106 in February 1984 had a report about Dan Inosanto and his Academy at Marina del Rey in California. It was sent in by Bob Breen, a former Karate instructor who 'went over' to JKD/Kali from the first moment he saw Sifu Dan Inosanto move! Here are three pictures from the report.

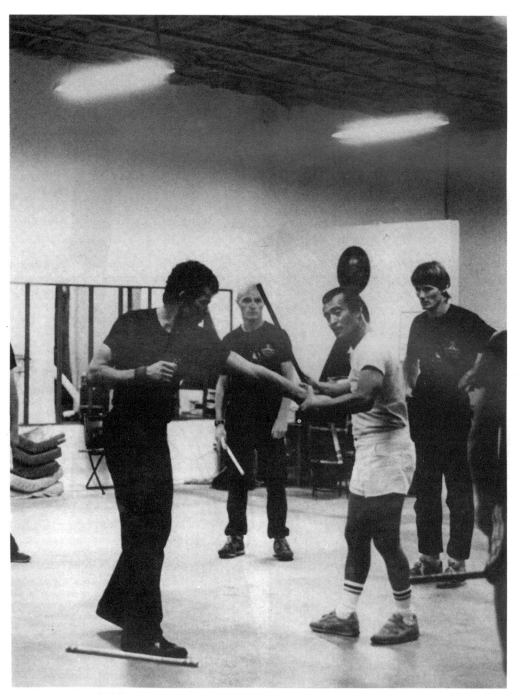

Bob Breen looks on (centre) as Sifu Inosanto demonstrates a disarm.

Poster of Bruce Lee looks down on the well stocked dojo as students go through empty hand drills.

Inosanto allows his arms to be locked up as Bob counters with single stick.

Bruce Lee as an Inspiration

Someone once referred to what Bruce Lee had left behind him as a legacy. His book is part of it, his films are part of it, and his pupils are part of it too. But as a man who inspired and still inspires hundreds of thousands of young men, and a smaller number of young women, many of whom are in a sense lost in the chaos of the life of today, it seems to me that more could be made of that legacy than has been made to date.

What I mean is that something of better quality, of a higher standard, could be produced in the film world for instance. The sudden death of Bruce Lee, which took everyone completely by surprise, caused a rush, a hasty attempt to produce some memorial to him, probably for purposes of gain rather than anything else. This is not said in a critical way, but simply as a statement of likely fact.

From the laughable works of the journalists struggling with the concepts of Kung fu to the "Silent Flute" itself, we do not see much of the deeper side. None of the millions of fans knew Bruce Lee at all. Like many mass media heroes he represents something; it is not Bruce Lee brushing his teeth in the evening that people rave about after all. It is something about his statement, his life and its expression which appeals. The fans feel a certain kinship with this. Again like other heroes they feel that Lee is speaking for them, trying to make utterances through word, and more through physical action, which they cannot make on such a massive scale. "Silent Flute" was a commendable effort at the time. But as someone once said, "It needs more work on it."

"The Tao of Jeet Kune Do" book was not exactly a book, as we have seen; not something which had he been alive Bruce Lee would have put his name to in that form. It was a compendium of notes. People took it because it was more or less all there was, and something is better than nothing. So when I say that something deeper could be provided in the shape of a film, I mean something over which time is spent, and suitable people are used to write a script and screenplay.

In this respect I can only recall again "The Seven Samurai", and "Dersu Uzala", Kurosawa's powerful and touching film about the encounter between a Russian soldier and a Siberian shaman. The epic "Godfather"

parts one and two also spring to mind as films which combine violence with masterly plotting and dialogue, camera work and editing. The care and attention given to this type of film is the kind needed to make a film based on Bruce Lee's life. Not on all his life, of course, but on those aspects of his life which fans and followers are touched in a way and to an extent one dare say that they do not understand themselves.

It is not what is overt about his life which is the more interesting and important, but rather it is what lies behind the overt life. There are plainly enormous tensions, caused by contradictions within the man. It is a big challenge to face the sayings of Zen or Taoism and at the same time build up your physique and push it to the limits. This latter type of effort on the face of it goes agains the Taoist idea of letting things be. On the other hand the nature of the Tao, so elusive, you can never put your finger on it, is echoed in the transformations that Carradine undergoes in "The Silent Flute", a role which Lee himself elected to play. Each time the hero thinks he has conquered, or "put his finger on it", the conquered man turns up in yet another guise.

Another facet of the picture is the comments Lee made when he had faced a challenge and won; it was not the winning which concerned him but the way he had won. He was nothing if not critical of himself. The pressures of meeting the demands of film studios must also have clashed at times with his own ideals and the messages that he was receiving from his readings of different philosophical teachings related to the Ways. To be engaged in many things requires a lot of energy, and one can only feel sympathy for a man who was trying to do so much in so little time. One cannot help wondering if Lee, the teacher, in fact needed a teacher himself. Not so much a martial arts teacher as a Zen or Taoist teacher who might have been able to bring him into alignment with the many aspects of his life, pulling in different directions.

So part of the inspiration of Lee is the fact that he tried, and tried and tried again. If at first you don't succeed... In my own experiences in life, I spent twelve years or so as a school teacher. It often seemed to me that much more use could be made of subjects which boys and girls are easily interested in, such as martial arts, games and dancing and their possible connection with more academic subjects. I had once put on a short play at one school, using mainly children from immigrant parents as well as the "native" English. Most of these children were not up to scratch academically. The district was poor and run down. Yet I found when they heard about the idea of pretending to be Vikings and ancient Britons that they responded very well. They had no difficulty with learning lines, making toy shields and swords and pretending to be the characters they played. They chanted simple chants I had made up for them. The play was a tremendous thing for them. One of the girls in the play was supposed to be ultra shy. Yet, she stood up at the beginning of the performance and spoke her lines without batting an eye, without any hesitation. I was a newcomer to the school and some of the teachers who had been there for years were frankly surprised. In the 6th issue of K.O.A., May/June 1967, after the brief article featuring Sean Connery and Tetsuro Tamba in the martial arts scenes from "You Only Live Twice", I put in the following editor's paragraphs. I was only young, and the article shows it, and our type-setting in those days was something below professional standard as we were, like some Hong Kong film makers, on a shoe-string budget:

Budo in Education

Paul H. Crompton

"Part two of an article concerning the possible uses of Budo in education, By "Budo" we simply mean the arts of Judo, Karate, Aikido and Kendo.

The last article spoke of a "need for a discipline which coordinates the entire boy or girl." Japanese fencing, Kendo, has a great deal to offer in this respect.

It incorporates technique, respect, etiquette, ritual, exercise, achievement. If we take the second of these points, respect, we find that this is a quality which is disappearing from the educational scene at an alarming rate. The Kendo teacher is of course superior in skill to his pupils and, they respect this side of him at least. So many children at schools to-day have an insecure background which makes them want to 'try it on' with the teacher to make sure that there is someone who can firmly deal with them and so give them a sense of a security which they lack at home. Given the chance to try their skill in at a 'contact art such as Kendo, they may experience a strong sense of security in

meeting and 'crossing swords' with a Kendo teacher.

Etiquette plays a big part in the practice of Kendo, and though it may be simply an outward obedience to a ritual series of movements and expressions, it has a rationale which is easily understood and explained. Children are notorious at certain ages for wanting to be told what to do, and for liking ritual. This is another strong point in favour of Kendo.

There is plenty of physical exercise in Kendo as in all the Budo arts, the strong shoulder and arm movements being good for breathing and circulation. Many of the movements are performed on the ball of the foot, thus strengthening the legs and cultivating a strong sense of balance.

If there is a problem you throw money at it and it will go away(?)

EXAMS

A system of 'exams and prizes' exists in Budo, but it is unique in that it is not based solely on intellectual knowledge, style, winning contests or technical ability. All these points, and also correct attitude, are taken into account at a 'grading'. Modern educationalists move further and further away from the 'examination system' and more towards an all-round assessment of the candidate based on past record as well as exam. results. In Budo this already exists. Thus, the pupil who is physically weaker but equal in skill in Judo for example will be given credit for his skill even though he may lose more contests than a stronger, more athletically inclined opponent.

In my first school I made a point of playing football with the boys, and when the snow came I threw snowballs, was snowballed and 'scragged' the boys as they tried to 'scrag' me. This brought a much closer teacher -pupil relationship, particularly as the boys were mostly from homes where it was impossible for them to live, for a variety of reasons. In Budo there is obviously, repeated physical contact of a strong, robust kind, which assures the pupil that the teacher really is there, that he is just like you really, not just a walking encyclopaedia and that he is struggling to improve, just as you are, and does not speak from some remote mountain top, expecting you to do the things which you have never seen him strive to do.

Now, some thirty plus years later, attitudes have changed and there is much more interchange in school curricula. Yet, there could be more. In England and perhaps in other countries, we take the view that if there is a problem you throw money at it and it will go away. In our National Health Service, there is little attention paid to preventive medicine. Measures such as teaching Tai Chi or something similar to the elderly would cost peanuts compared with the vast drug bills. I have taught it to very elderly people with good results and so have others.

In Education, to take someone like Bruce Lee and find ways of relating his martial skills and attitudes to a school subject is not a difficult undertaking and one which I am sure could pay big dividends, if finance is your metaphor of choice. An intelligent and dedicated teacher could do it. In this way, some of the enthusiastic allegiance which a youngster has to a star or athlete or astronaut could be linked to school subjects. Biology/physiology relates to physical training for example. Though bombarded by a great deal of media rubbish, youngsters must still be relatively open to such steps. Isolated examples of teachers taking such steps exist, but what might be a better idea is to set up a whole educational body which would study this prospect, throw money *and* brains at it. If only money were the answer, then the U.S.A.

would have the best educated population in the world. I don't believe this is the case. Just remember how diligently a young fan or collector goes about his hobby. Without prompting he will search, obtain and classify any subject. He may be inattentive in the classroom, play truant, cause trouble, but when it comes to his hobby he is completley different. Use can be made of this. At an older level of education, the book sources which Lee found for many of his sayings and notes could be cited to school youngsters. Many of them had a religious or philosophical background and as in most schools today religion plays a very small part, and ideas from religious sources are scant, the inspiration of someone such as Lee could be used to awaken interest. Of course the onus for all this inspiration lies on the shoulders of the teachers. But the subject could be studied as a means.

One reads in the press about violence in schools, and how it has reached almost unmanageable proportions. In England a few years ago a school master, a head teacher, was stabbed by a pupil in the playground and died. This appalling event led to much coverage in the media. My own view is, for what it's worth, is that once again a well funded body should be started, to study how the physical and emotional energy behind such violence can be channelled into something else. Kung Fu films, Bruce Lee films, released enormous energy in the youth of the day. It was pent up energy, clearly there waiting to come out. Bruce Lee "spoke" for this energy, not just for Chinese Kung Fu. His films said, more or less, that there were disciplined ways in which this energy could be combined with intellectual studies.

The authorities in Britain devised for example the"short, sharp shock" treatment in which young tearaways would be compelled to undergo virtual military discipline. In the United States, similar efforts were made, and others used ranch style, cowboy experiences to channel the energies of youngsters and give them something, a horse, to care about. Some of these endeavours were more successful than others, but my own impression is that something on a national scale is needed, to bring the whole subject into focus.

Why were fans so eager to follow Lee? He was not just a hero, but something of a father figure, however youthful; an authority figure who did not merely refer to books and mathematics. Millions of kids in the western world now have no live-at-home father. Small wonder that they feel lost and frustrated. When will governments get the

The best fighters do not give way to anger *(Tao Te Ching)*

message and do what is necessary? Part of the difficulty can be demonstrated and found in the events of Bruce Lee's own life. I mean that in the sense that he was trying to undertake lines of endeavour which were in a sense incompatible. Martial arts, philosophy, film making, teaching, being a father and being a husband. This requires a virtual superman.

So in one man the aim is verging on the impossible. But a government, an educational ministry, is not one man, but many men and women. The difficulty here is different. The difficulty is that each man and each woman is usually concerned with one thing, unlike Lee, not many. And the skills of adminstration, or teaching mathematics, or being physically very able and fit, are not often found in one and the same person. Yet it is this type of person, in whom more than one talent is combined, that is needed for setting up new approaches to youngsters. Either that, or a close cooperation between two or more persons who together make up such a combination. Together they could study not how to teach each of their individual skills or understanding, but how to combine them into a whole, so that those sides of a youngster's development could be simultaneously addressed.

Moving on from there, we find in educational establishments that often there is rivalry between existing departments, for recognition, for funds and promotion and so forth. This is not in the interests of the school children or youths. The solution proposed here needs a combined effort; one in which the government would have to make sure that rivalry, funds, promotion and so forth were treated in an even handed way. Then, if this were done, teaching would truly become a vocation. The trouble is that when someone has a vocation, the authorities take advantage of this and milk it for all they are worth. In Britain the nursing profession is another example, as is caring for the elderly; anything where a person's feelings and inner convictions are concerned gets a financial raw deal. Virtue may be its own reward, as the saying goes, but it does not pay the rent.

A last but by no means final point concerns the general decline in physical skills in society. On the following page is a table showing how and in what ways this has come about since roughly the beginning of the industrial revolution. Maybe future social historians will see martial arts, along with other "pastimes" as the last gasp of the technologically afflicted human body. As the Terminator might have put it:

"The machines have taken over."

The human body is being reduced to its final skill:
Button Pushing.

Skill then...

Skill now...

Skill then...	Skill now...
Walking, running, climbing, etc.	Trains, planes and automobiles
Cycling..	Typing and faxing
Manually written letters.......................	Telephoning and e-mailing
Visiting...	Using the above means
Cooking with all its skills:...................	Prepared food, fast food, sliced
Preparing vegetables, fish, etc.	bread, polluted food, pre-selected
Baking bread, cutting bread	food
Cutting down trees by hand................	Mechanical saws
Sawing up trees by hand....................	Mechanical saws
Sawing, chiselling, gouging wood.....	Automatic bits
Making holes in wood - hand drills...	Automatic drills
Putting in nails and screws by hand.	Automatic screwdrivers
Wood and metal work by hand...........	Automatic tools in general
Washing clothes by hand...................	Washing machines
Washing dishes by hand.....................	Dishwashers
Playing games with children..............	Television, video games, computers
Inventing one's own amusements......	Cinema, television, electric toys
Craftsmanship in general flourishing	Craftsmanship disappearing
Making substances manually from original ingredients.............................	Pre-chosen, pre-mixed, pre-every-thing
Family doctor, bedside manner..........	Blanket prescription of drugs
Fewer drugs, more preventive...........	More drugs, less preventive

This list is not exhaustive. It is not an indictment of inventions and technological and medical breathroughs. It is simply a presentation of a few facts which add up to a weakening in the role of the physical body in modern life. Ultimately the body expresses what is inside. No body, no expression. The body produces most of the energy we need to live. Even the energy we receive from elsewhere, indirectly so to speak, the body processes in some form or other. It is not an exaggeration to say the body is gradually declining. Medicine neglects the preventive side in the elderly, which should be geared to keeping joints moving and circulation alive. It is not a question of the means being unavailable, but somehow the "will" is lacking. Maybe it is being sapped by the ease of button pressing. It is not an exaggeration either to say that figures such as Bruce Lee can inspire people to find the will not to reverse the trend, but to preserve the life of the human body.

The Jan Wright Story

Jan Wright is one of the great well known unknowns of the English martial arts world. Amazingly, he had researched the same One Inch Power Punch as had Bruce Lee, completely as we say, off his own bat.

Wright teaches what he knows.

Jan Wright went to boarding school as a youngster and there he met many Asian students who had a background in martial arts. This was over forty years ago. Leaving school, he continued to study martial arts, being interested in Wing Chun and Aikido. When the Kung Fu craze hit his small town where he had his own club, membership leaped from 10 to 100 in a few days. When Bruce Lee's films arrived the demand for training in Kung Fu was so great that he could not accommodate everyone. Then, he writes, "instant instructors appeared ready to make a fast buck".

At the Crewe Carnival, he had arranged to hold a martial arts day. About one hundred martial arts clubs of all types had been invited to attend and show what they were doing. These included Karate clubs as well as Miss Lee's Tai Chi students and Jujitsu practitioners. He was surprised when many of them failed to appear. On enquiring at a local Karate club, he found out that on the day some tough guys from a Liverpool club had turned up, threatening to beat up anyone who appeared at the Carnival. Read into this what you will.

Over the years, Wright had questioned many martial arts styles and in the end designed his own, based on modified Wing Chun. He then corresponded with James DeMile and Jesse Glover and was "amazed to learn that my style in many ways mirrored Bruce's style, right down to my one inch punch, which I had measured for the Guiness Book of Records as 105.75 lbs. per square inch". This measurement was made at a technical college, Dane Bank College.

He points out that there is a difference between creating a style and merely adding a mixture of moves from various arts. A style must have a fundamental aspect such as the shortest distance between two points. But once it does, then this fundamental aspect can automatically restrict the style.

He too remembers the con trick which was perpetrated by some German entrepreneur and relates how he had invited James DeMile to come over to teach in England, as the first pupil of Bruce Lee to do so. Wright was contacted by a German instructor who asked if DeMile could go to his club. DeMile agreed and for a month the course was advertised in Germany. Lot of people paid good money. James DeMile flew from Hawaii to Germany and arrived at the man's address to find it was a prison. What happened to the money, and where the 'instructor' went is a mystery. (See page 178)

When Full Contact Karate appeared, Wright's student entrant knocked out his Karate style opponent in one second. Wright went on to develop one move which could finish a fight fast. One of his students adopted this move, trained at it, and went a long way, winning all his fights using just this one move. Wright still runs a martial arts club, and his website is:

http://www.mwright.u.net.com where details of his style appear.

VIEW OF BRUCE LEE

He regards Bruce Lee as still the most important martial artist ever to have lived, and states that his art is still not widely understood. "Bruce's art has suffered from people making money out of it, with many people claiming to teach it". He points out that most of the martial arts we have today were invented in very different times, when conditions of life were unimaginably foreign to us. He believes that we should have an art which suits the type of person we are and the type of body we have, although the body can be modified. "Bruce Lee could however have done what he did, even if he had been built like a Sumo wrestler".

Wright's own ideas of martial arts include his love of Aikido. He considers that what the founder of Aikido used in the way of techniques to *illustrate* his basic concept of turning an attacker's force back on himself, have been turned into laws by many of his followers. What should be a means has become an end in itself. Speaking to Jan Wright after many years about this very thing, I had to agree, but at the same time we both have had the experience of seeing very clearly that this is a difficult thing for a beginner to grasp, and he needs the basic techniques of Aikido or another chosen method as a starting point.

What Bruce Lee arrived at, the idea of experimentation, exploration, of using what works and what is useful, presents the majority of martial arts students with a very difficult approach. And perhaps it is one, in all fairness, which they do not want to tackle. This consideration stands beside the fact of the the big differences between the man and woman poised on the brink of the millenium, in the arena of modern life, and the martial artists of the past who maybe trained for six hours a day and then did manual labour of some kind the rest of the time.

Jan himself works at a very important job in a bank, teaches the bank staff in the lunch hour and at age 52 says, "My style is going through changes as I get older... no longer can I kick so high or move so fast... but now I have experience and a relaxed power that youth denied me. My style is now more internal than before, focusing on the use of Ki (Chi, Qi) and this new relaxed power".

The arts are like a journey, "which starts out as a way to defend yourself or to show off, but soon becomes the search for final truth. Now I have no need to prove that I am big and tough, the battle is no longer with my opponent but with myself. I am aware that sooner or later there will be a final battle that I cannot t win; maybe then the mysteries of life that I have searched for may become clear. Wright is concerned that what he has discovered and worked on in the way of technique will be lost when he goes. He recognises that others have faced the same prospect. In this connection he recalled an incident in which the founder of Aikido promised to teach his students some new moves. Eagerly his students waited and watched as he demonstrated for them for a full hour. When he had finished the students protested that during the whole sixty minutes the master had performed the same technique over and over again. What they had seen was merely what they *could* see. They could see only the familiar physical movements. They could not see the variations in the use of Ki (Chi,Qi) employed by their teacher. Wright sees analogies with his own experience, and reflects that the block he did twenty years ago is not the block he does today; it looks the same but the content is different.

As any martial artist connected with films knows, this subtle distinction does not sell films. The audience want to be wowed by dynamic action. Wright recalls that in the Christian Bible and in other respected writings the simplicity inherent in the flow of Ki is described. The words may change, but the meaning is the same. He reminds us of Bruce Lee's famous words:

> **Don't watch the finger** (pointing at the moon),
> **Or you will miss all the heavenly wonder.**

In a letter to KOA about this time, Jan Wright said, "No one can really teach Jeet Kune Do. Lee *was* Jeet Kune Do, and most of his students don't even use the words now, (1977). DeMile uses Wing Chun Do, and Don Inosanto uses Kali... You see, Lee trained every student differently, according to his strengths and weaknesses, and if he had trained me it would come out the same as what I call my style... Chi Sau Tao."

There are thousands of styles in Mainland China. Bruce Lee grew up in Hong Kong. Is it fair to ask the question, "Would he have had the same attitude to the 'classical mess' if he had been exposed to a much wider experience of these styles?" It must be a difficult question for fans to face?

CHINA is a very BIG COUNTRY

During the period we are looking at, when Bruce Lee's popularity was at its height, Mainland China was a "closed" country. Most people could not simply waltz over there in search of the Shaolin temple! During the 1950's the government had begun collating martial arts styles into groups and drawing up syllabuses for training. They called upon various experts to help them with this. Since that time, the authorities have continued to do similar things, ever expanding the programmes and bringing new methods and standards to the fore.

One of the overseas publication representatives for China, if not *the* one, was the Peace Book Company, which distributed pro-government literature, revised literature, Chairman Mao's famous thoughts, new People's Dance information and many other things. They also produced a very attractive wall poster of Tai Chi showing the now famous 24 Step Beijing Form or Simplified Tai Chi. But on the whole they were pretty sparing in their release of martial arts literature of a practical nature. "Chi(qi)" for instance was a big "no-no" word.

This meant that westerners and perhaps Hong Kong Chinese martial artists, did not all know the unbelievable wealth of skill and knowledge which still existed on the mainland. We had Chinese emigrants, Hong Kong and Taiwan (Formosa) to go on. K.O.A. tried to get hold of more information and books on the martial arts in China but the people in Beijing were not forthcoming. We understood it was a political thing, an attitude to pre-revolutionary subject matter, but we could not get our heads round it. Plainly, we did not have the right thoughts!

Time passed, then long after Bruce Lee had passed away and the roots of JKD had been planted, its ideals published and its teachers travelled to the four corners of the earth with their message, the bamboo curtain began to lift. People were amazed at what they began to find. Some westerners went for a month and stayed for years. They had found teachers and styles beyond their dreams.

In addition to Tai Chi teachers, because Tai Chi became very fashionable, not to say useful and popular. But in addition there was Hsing-I and Pakua, and subdivision after subdivision of these styles, and Drunken style, Monkey style, Bear, and so on, as dozen after dozen of methods were "discovered". Eventually some American Chinese martial artists and their cameramen were allowed into the country and wandered far and wide collecting on film, without let or hindrance so it seemed, hour after hour of martial arts demonstrations.

These varied from old Shaolin monks who were suffering from old age, to superfit Wushu, or traditional "Kung Fu", young to middle-aged experts, whose level of fitness Bruce Lee himself would have admired. I saw much of this film myself, was taught for months by one of the younger experts, and in getting round to putting this book together could not help linking what I saw and experienced to the Bruce Lee legend. The exhibition of Drunken style is almost awesome and the power of some of the Hsing-I almost frightening. The speed of the Pakua movement too shows an amazing control of footwork. Not many western martial artists or Chinese martial artists come up to the level of physical control and power seen in these tapes. Bruce Lee did not see them. He had Hong Kong, Wing Chun and Grandmaster Yip Man as his examples. When he went to the United States he had the expatriate Chinese of San Francisco, but not the cream of the "old country". He had his martial arts pupils, his film star pupils and admirers, his film studio business and television, the American Karate and Taekwondo scene, but what he did not have were the roots, where it all began. When you watch these tapes you have an inkling of this, and it is no "classical mess".

What it underlines for me is the old saying that there is always someone better than you, who understands better than you, who has done what you have done, and more, and that there is nothing new under the sun. It is what is written elsewhere in this book, that Bruce Lee at a critical time of his life needed not so much a teacher as a mentor, an older and wiser source of advice. As you go through the tapes referred to, and others, you see that the advice was there, somewhere, inside all this Kung Fu wisdom. It is like seeing a film of the United States, or travelling there. On the surface there is the good old U.S.A. and then beneath it, and all around it there is the sense of older, vanished peoples, so old that the land itself seems to be impregnated with the sweat of their cultures. Similar things could be said of course about Australia, where in a way the modern Aussies have only just arrived, even though their generations can be measured through several centuries.

The quite separate question but closely linked with this one is who Bruce Lee met as he grew up; what sort of people were they, what calibre were they, what were their attitudes and how much of all this rubbed off on Lee and so got up his nose that he became associated with the phrase "classical mess"? In turn the phrase got up the nose of many traditional Chinese. I suspect that many of the best simply ignored it, putting it down to youthful exuberance on Lee's part. Questions like these have been cursorily addressed and dismissed with little thought in most writings I have seen. What the reasons for this are I don't know and don't wish to speculate about. They may be private reasons on the part of the writers, they may be commercial reasons and for instance they may be reasons of simple ignorance. It is not my concern. I am interested in the question, rather than the reasons for it not being answered. When compiling this book I made some open and respectful enquiries in the United States and had few favourable or helpful responses. Everyone has reasons.

SYSTEMS

We know from many articles and books that Bruce Lee avidly sought methods of increasing his physical performance and energy levels. One might even be tempted to say he was addicted to this quest. In going to the United States he was in a country where systems of body building, energy building, muscle control and super-new systems related to these topics are in abundance.   Some of them pay scant regard to the overall or long term health of the student. They promise quick results and speak about the human organism as if it were a motor car or plumbing system. In this respect they have something in common with miracle diet and health regimes. They do this either through ignorance or for reasons of marketing to a gullible public.

So, gullibility figures prominently in some types of advertising of systems. Apart from the famous remark about suckers, "There's one born every minute," there is the remark made by a local barber which he made to a customer and which I overheard when about eleven years old and waiting for a haircut in the barber's shop. Their conversation was about baldness and cures for baldness. In the end, the barber said, "If there was a cure for baldness, the Duke of Windsor wouldn't be losing his hair." Why this sentence remained in my available memory I don't know, but it shows that if some of the promises made in many advertisements were true then wealthy or famous people would be able to obtain the results promised very easily; money no problem.

In other types of advertising, the promised results can be obtained but at the expense of the health of the user, either at the time or later. For instance in the recent past the sexual performance enhancing drug Viagra has apparently caused deaths among users with latent or existing health problems. There is more than one example!

Other types of advertising make the user permanently dependent on the product or the sellers, either for health or addictive reasons. So, in brief, advertising can give you problems. In the United States, Bruce Lee would have been bombarded with literature offering methods and courses in systems. He had graduated from the systems of classical Chinese Kung fu, but was now into the systems of American fitness products. What most of these products suffer from is that they take the short term view; they are aimed at quick results and rely on over simplification. One such over simplfied view is that everyone needs to become flexible and should do flexibility exercises. Such advice does not take into account a very simple and scientifically proven fact. This is that the same does not apply to everyone. In dance training at the highest professional level it is known that flexibility training for some types of physique should be kept to a minimum. Some physiques are flexible-prone already, and flexibility exercises can easily reduce performance. Other physiques can really benefit and others need just a moderate amount of such training. So, one cannot help wondering if Bruce Lee was over-impressed by modern products. Maybe he wasn't.

In China, among the many classical systems of health and strength improvement there are ones which aim at long term, gradual build up of "chi" or energy reserves. Their chief drawback, as far as the training regimes of Bruce Lee are concerned, is that they are slow and gradual. They take a lifetime view, whereas the star seemed to want to be right on top of things all the time, where his body was concerned. He gave the impression of wanting results right now. This is understandable given his dual life style: star and martial artist. We read of long, long hours spent in filming and dealing with problems connected with filming and all the stress which must go with it. We read of the need for him to be instantly ready to perform a movement sequence many times, each time striving to be perfect. We read of him trying to deal with the financial side of the film world. This type of lifestyle is not compatible with maintaining the level of excellence which he set himself. He would have benefited more from a permanent, entirely responsible agent who could have handled all those things for him. Conditions at the time dictated otherwise.

In China at the time there were excellent teachers of more than one style who could have encouraged and helped Bruce Lee in his quest for the martial arts goals he had set himself. The bamboo curtain did not help. There were others who understood health and physical development but the same problem applied. My own view is that Bruce Lee, in turning his back on his own martial arts inheritance, prematurely, acted against his own best interests as a martial artist. This may have been due to his success in show business as much as anything else. By appearing at tournaments in the U.S.A. and showing his Power Punch and other feats, he put himself in a position where he had to pursue contact with the public, which includes martial artists, because his demonstrations had provoked them. When his films achieved the successes they did there was no turning back. He was riding a tiger and could not dismount. Like any champion, he could only strive to stay at the top.

What I have written here may not be popular, I know, but I wonder if Bruce Lee had-been under the guidance of a venerable and respected teacher from the old country he might still be with us today. He thought he was standing on his own martial arts feet at an early age, when most martial artists are still in their martial arts adolescence. He impressed, he was idolised. This is not good juju for steady development.

I used to hear from readers of K.O.A. from the United States who had it in for Bruce Lee. They were people who criticised him strongly, and attempted to detract from his achievements. As a magazine publisher I ignored their contributions as they were soaked in prejudice and ill feeling. At the same time, it does a star or a martial arts athlete no good to hear and read nothing but praise and idolatry. What would make the most interesting reading of all, and I doubt if we shall never see it published, is a truly critical assessment of the man and his methods, compiled from in depth, truthful and no holds barred interviews with all the relevant people, put into prose by an impartial writer. Any offers?

Note: not everyone warmed to President Nixon, but one publication devoted to subjects such as chi (qi)) noted that it was after the detente which followed his visit to China and much publicised interview with Chairman Mao that Chinese attitudes towards traditional subjects began visibly to relax.

Bodhidharma - the Saint of Shaolin

Chinese martial artists regard the Buddhist teacher, Bodhidharma, as the progenitor of Shaolin temple martial arts. Tradition says that the physical demands of his meditation methods were too much for the Chinese monks so he devised a series of exercises to improve their strength. These exercises and the regimes which followed are said to be the foundation of martial arts training in the Shaolin temple or monastery.

Of course, not all Chinese martial arts stemmed from there, but the place and the teacher have a central position in the traditions. If that is so, then we can fairly say that the origins of those arts concerned were focussed on Buddhist enlightenment, not on fighting. If the analogy is not too far fetched we can say it can be compared with the orginal aim of scientists discovering how to split the atom, compared with the application of their methods to make an atomic bomb. It is an old story of human endeavour starting out in one direction and then heading in the opposite one.

Bodhidharma's ancestry is a matter for debate. He is seen as an Indian, a Persian, a South Indian Prince, but first and foremost a Buddhist. He made the long voyage to China, at the request of his teacher, Prajnaratna, and after an audience with the Emperor Wu-ti, went north to Loyang. In the Sung mountain he saw the Shaolin monastery and remained there until he died, "facing the wall" in meditation. His chief disciple was Hui-ke, who laid the foundations of Chan Buddhism (Sanskrit name Dhyanna). Chan was taken to Japan where it is known as Zen. Contrary to what many people believe, Bodhidharma was not the first notable Buddhist in China. Among the others were Paramartha and Kumarajiva, and at the famous White Horse monastery, translations of Buddhist texts into Chinese had been taking place for at least three centuries.

What happened during the translations was that the renderings were by no means faithful to the original Indian texts, but were adaptations infused with Chinese subject matter which made them acceptable to Chinese people. Elements of Taoism moved into the new Chinese versions and gradually Chinese Buddhism emerged, most enduringly in the Chan tradition, where the spirit of Lao-tze can clearly be seen.

Parallels with the development of martial arts are irresistible. Martial arts which came to China were developed along Chinese lines. Taoism seeped into them, traditional Chinese medicine seeped into them, and Moslem martial arts, which still exist today in China, added to the score, in addition to the prominent influence of Buddhism from the Shaolin temple.

One does not have to lean too far backwards to bring Bruce Lee into this picture. Depending on how far you are prepared to go, you could say that both his criticism of the "classical mess", and the ones who unquestioningly perpetuated it both belong in the same barrel. This is because the original purpose of martial arts was to stop fighting!

In the seminal ancient book, "The Art of War", the highest skill a general can have is to end a war or battle before it starts. The second highest is to end it as soon as possible with the smallest number of casualties, and so forth. To preserve a classical martial arts tradition on the basis that it is the best and should never be changed is clearly a mistake, because conditions always vary. But to condemn classical tradition outright is no help either; you throw the baby out with the bath water.

In spite of the classical mess saying which hangs around Bruce Lee's neck like an albatross, he is to be commended because in spite of it he never ceased to try out new methods and new approaches. If what James DeMile is quoted as saying is true, that the most important thing for Lee was to win, then Lee's aim was on a lower level than his approach. It is not too fine a point. A scientist who stays true to the ideal of continuing to experiment, no matter if the experiment destroys years of earlier work, is admired and commended by all. But if the motive behind such an approach is just to be better than anyone else, then the motive dilutes the process, spoils it in a sense.

A Zen Buddhist's advice in such a situation might be to "kill the motive", and thereby purify or bring understanding to the man, or woman. If such advice were the foundation of martial arts, in reality, the situation which Bruce Lee disliked so intensely would not have existed. But it is not, and though no Bodhidharma, no Hui-ke, Bruce Lee did succeed in bringing many Chinese traditionalists to a salutary halt with his Zen-like shout.

John Saxon's remark about the irony of making Lee himself into a myth, and the pos- sibility of converting his attitude of constant experimentation into a creed would be a true reversal of intention. Dyed in the wool traditionalists could point a finger at him and say, "Welcome to the club...".

With Bruce Lee gone, there is no possibility of his refining his motive.   Both sides should be reconciled by the saying which Lee himself quoted,

It is like a finger pointing at the moon.

(I did not want to be part of the "classical mess"!)

In their own way, the pictures at the top of this page spell "conclusion". I wanted to leave them with no explanation but I did not have the heart to do so. In the martial arts world, everyone works out his or her own shorthand for learning and doing. So one person's shorthand might look like that pictorial webding font at the top of the page to someone else. Unintelligible except to a five year old code breaker!

In putting this book together I could have consulted and dragged in all the standard books on Bruce Lee, juggled them around and put them out as one more "new" book on the famous star. This would have been a waste of paper and a waste of money for anyone who had read the other books. Instead, by comparing past and present views, thoughts and memories of K.O.A. magazine about the phenomenon of Bruce Lee, without taking sides with any particular one, I hope that something fresh has appeared for you the reader.

At the present time, martial arts is facing a revival after some years of falling interest. Chinese Wushu and arts from countries other than Japan are responsible for this, I believe. For the moment, 'Budo' is not in accord with what many martial artists are looking for; (Jujutsu seems to be an exception); Budo's day may return. This may be because whilst the heirs of JKD have felt free to explore, the heirs of Budo have not nearly so much. Today it is in the air to find out and get something together for yourself. There are more and more synthesised styles, where people who have been training for a long time have put together their own version of a martial art. As was noted in the Introduction, this is a reflection of society as a whole. Similarly, more and more 'versions' of 'JKD' are appearing, in what is a further expression of the desire to synthesise. Whether it is a desire, or more likely an irresistible force of our times, is hard to decide.

As I looked through the past, in the form of photos, letters, articles, faxes, messages jotted down on scraps of paper, videos, books and magazines, then made my own notes, typed paragraphs, corrected and re-corrected, faces and incidents from the past would leap back at me. Then an incident, and the feelings and thoughts experienced at the time would all stream into mind. Sometimes, I would be transported back twenty or more years, to when for instance during a phone conversation, a martial artist said, "And if you say that again I'll come down to Fulham Road and smash you!" The vibes as he spoke shook the telephone lines. Then the phrase of another peace loving martial artist returned to stand beside the first salutary memory. When he disliked some-one he would say, "I'll beat you to a piss." This was not about a race to the uri-nals! No one knew exactly what this threat meant, but the look in his eyes sup-plemented the words. The occasional apprehension I felt at the time returned and reminded me of the emotional effect that the boom period had on everyone. Feelings of inadequacy, of rage, of the desire to prove oneself, were all prominent at that time, and for some people were focussed through martial arts. As edi-tor of a magazine I was the nearest thing readers had to a live punchbag or maki-wara or Wing Chun dummy; thankfully figuratively speaking.

One day a really huge, and I mean huge, Irishman came into the K.O.A. shop. We were talking about martial arts and to demonstrate a point I put my arm on his arm. "Don't you touch me!!!" came the booming voice from somewhere up close to the ceiling. I felt I ought to do as he said... The phone was most readers' favourite weapon. I would be informed, in no uncertain tone of voice, that this person or that person was a load of rubbish and why had we printed something about him, because blah, blah, blah... I never developed a thick enough skin to shrug these verbal assaults off. Sometimes at the end of the day I would be shattered and would ruefully reflect that this was the downside of Bruce Lee's success.

On the other side, some martial artists were courtesy and restraint itself, and made me feel that somehow the messages had got through to these people and they were a credit to whatever style they followed. The memories of those days would fill several books, telling as they do of the full gamut of human emotions and aspira-tions. We had our share of crooks. People shop lifted at the slightest opportunity. On one never to be forgotten occasion I took two martial artists out for a meal, with a friend of mine, had a pleasant time, accepted a large cheque, found it bounced and never managed to trace the man again. It was all part of the martial arts learn-ing curve. Though this has nothing to do with Mr. Lee, it was part of the expe-rience of life that he brought to me and many others, indirectly. My wife, my chil-dren, my friends and relatives, all felt the effects.

Another thing was the impact that Lee's success had on foreign instructors, mainly Chinese, Korean and Japanese. It did not apply to all of them but it did to many. For example, an instructor who, in his own country, would not have attracted much of a following would find that in England, Europe or the U.S.A. he was suddenly Master So-and-So, the famous teacher of Such-and-Such. If you met him, and if you followed the expectations of his English pupils, you were to virtually kiss the ground if not his feet. Usually I did not do this, but called him "Mr." and behaved with simple respect, explaining that I was not his pupil and merely a reporter. Secondly, some eastern teachers could not handle their own success. They knew that they were not really the masters of martial arts that their own English pupils made them out to be and, strangers in a strange land, they were nervous. They asked for large amounts of money for courses, amounts that sometimes boggled the mind. They did not in fact in many cases know what they could ask for. English people did not know what to expect to pay. They found out! It was all very strange, and some teachers made a great deal of cash.

Another human weakness surfaced during the boom - gullibility. Many students would believe almost anything if the teacher said it. Happily, as some English martial artists became better and better, they proved that what some teachers claimed to be the real McCoy was in fact rubbish. There was also a great deal of political in-fighting, with officials striving to get to the top of the pile, to be chairman of this organisation or president of that, or to be overall in charge of everyone else.

Throughout all these machinations, the enormous contradiction between what martial arts were supposed to be about, and the things people said and wrote they were about on the one hand, and what people did and said on the other, was overlooked. Some students found it too much and dropped out to do their own thing. Others joined in the game, and others just went with the flow.

Strangely, and for what it's worth, I feel closer to Bruce Lee and what he provoked, now that I am a much older man, than I did in my earlier years. I put this down to a certain degree of maturity in myself, but also because at the time I found it impossible to see him in anything like a true perspective. Too much was happening. So much hype, so much rubbish, so much money-grabbing, so much conmanship, on top of the genuine endeavours, that the man himself was obscured by it all. It is only now, some twenty-five years later, when things have calmed down so much, time and experience have elapsed, and I can feel a strong sympathy with a young man who lived through a typhoon of personal success. He tried manfully to keep his feet on the ground, but success made it hard for him to do so. The legacy of his life and martial arts testify to the existence of a most unusual human being deserving our sympathetic consideration rather than our blind adulation.

Some Of The Events In Bruce Lee's Life.
(Precise dates given where known.)

November 27th 1940 - born in San Francisco - parents Mr. & Mrs. Lee Hoi Chuen.

Winter 1941 - appears as a girl baby in "Golden Gate Girl" his first film role.

Winter 1941 - parents take him to Hong Kong, their home.

1947(?) - aged 6, second film part in "The Beginning of a Boy", Hong Kong.

1949(?) - aged 8, third film part where he is called Little Dragon. The name sticks. Becoming a young tearaway.

1953(?) - taken in hand by Catholic priest at school, Brother Henry Pang.

1953 - introduced to Yip Man's Wing Chun by William Cheung.

1959 - returns to America from Hong Kong and meets James Lee.

Spring 1963 - meets Linda Emery, his future wife, in Seattle.

September 1963 - turned down by draft board as unfit for military service!

Autumn 1963 - issues prospectus for his Gung Fu Institute.

July 1964 - demonstrates his Power Punch at Ed Parker's Long Beach tournament and meets James DeMile for the first time.

Summer 1964 - marries Linda.

1966/67 - thirty episodes of "Green Hornet" television series shown for first time.

1967 - memorable interview in "Black Belt" magazine; refers to himself in early life as a "young punk".

1969 - serious writing of "Silent Flute" begins.

1970 - on trip to Hong Kong is lionised by the public for his "Green Hornet" series.

1970(?) - "Longstreet" television series about to be produced.

1970 - injures back whilst weight training - bedridden for three months.

1970 - Run Run Shaw and Raymond Chow separate and Chow forms Golden Harvest. Chow signs Bruce Lee up to make two films.

July 1971 - flies to Bangkok via Hong Kong to start filming.

October 1971 - premiere of "Big Boss" in Hong Kong brings the house down. Plans for American television shelved.

1972 - "Fist of Fury" released.

1972 - "Way of the Dragon" released.

May 10th 1973 - Bruce Lee collapses at film studios and recovers; pronounced perfectly fit.

1973 - "Enter the Dragon" released.

July 20th 1973 - Bruce Lee's death in Queen Elizabeth hospital, Hong Kong.

A SELECTION OF MARTIAL ARTS PUBLICATIONS RELEVANT TO THIS ANTHOLOGY:

Bruce Lee Fighting Method - 4 volumes
Bruce Lee - the Man only I knew - Linda Lee
Bruce Lee's 1-3 inch Power Punch - James DeMile
Bruce Lee Nunchaku in Action
Bruce Lee: the Biography - Robert Clouse
Bruce Lee Story - Linda Lee
Bruce Lee: the Untold Story - CFW Publications
Chinese Gung fu: Philosophical Art of Self Defense - Bruce Lee
Jeet Kune Do - Art & Philosophy - Dan Inosanto
Jeet Kune Do - Entering to Trapping to Grappling - Larry Hartsell
Jeet Kune Do Kickboxing - Chris Kent/...Tackett
The Making of Enter the Dragon - Robert Clouse
The Tao of Jeet Kune Do - Bruce Lee

****

Karate Kata Training - Geir Store
Kata & Kumite for Karate - Chris Thompson

****

Breaking Power of Wing Chun - Austin Goh
Path to Wing Chun - Samuel Kwok
Wooden Dummy of Wing Chun - William Cheung

****

Basic Monkey Boxing - Richard Dean
Introduction to Shaolin Kung Fu - Wong Kiew Kit
Pak Mei Kung Fu - Ho Bun Un
Praying Mantis Kung Fu - Ho Bun Un

****

Savate: Boxe Francaise - Philip Reed/Richard Muggeridge

****

Spiritual Journey of Aikido - Huw Dillon
Tomiki Aikido - Dr. Ah Loi Lee

****

Elements of Tai Chi - Paul Crompton
Tai Chi Combat - Paul Crompton
Tai Chi Training in China - Howard Thomas

Publisher's Note:

If readers wish to pass on additional *helpful* information to be included in further editions of this book, write to the address below.

For information on martial arts books, videos...

Write, enclosing a stamped addressed envelope, or if outside this country send an international reply coupon, IRC, to:

PAUL H. CROMPTON LTD.,
& K.O.A. VIDEO,
94 Felsham Road, London, sw15 1dq.
England.